# EAGLES

## hell freezes over

contents



Transcribed by JOE DELORO, DALE TURNER and KENN CHIPKIN

Editor: Aaron Stang
Transcription Editor: Colgan Bryan



3N 0-89724-560-1

# get over it

Words and Music by
DON HENLEY and GLEN FREY

*Two gtrs. (seperate channels) arranged as one.

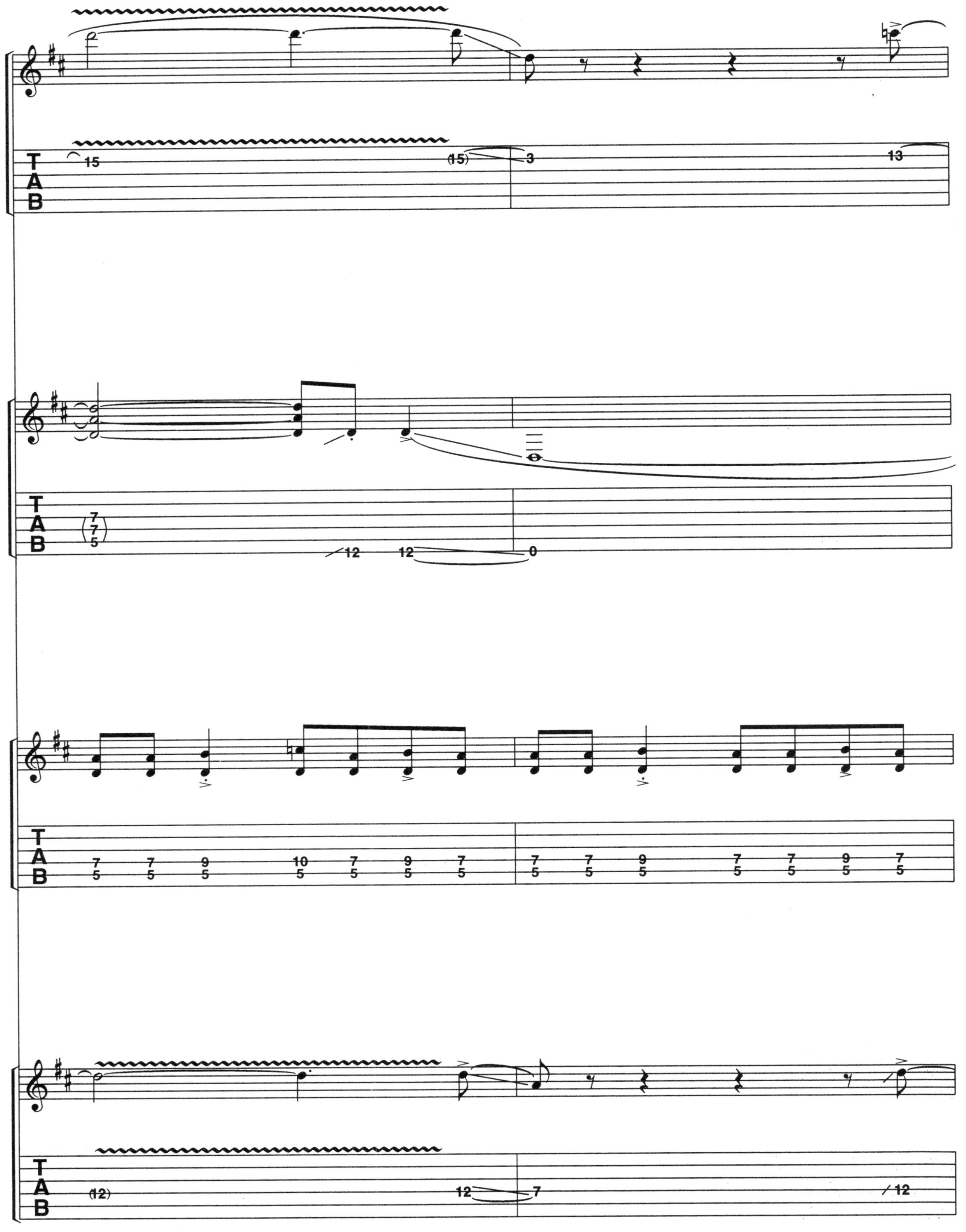

15
(15)
3
13
7
7
5
12
12
0
7
5
7
5
9
5
10
5
7
5
9
5
7
5
7
5
7
5
9
5
7
5
7
5
9
5
7
5
(12)
12
7
12

I
T
A
B
15
(15)
3
15
3
(0)
7
5
9
10
(12)
12
7

Verse:
D
turn on the tube and what do I see: a whole lot-ta peo-ple cry-in',
Gtr. 1
plucked throughout
Rhy. Fig. 1.
Gtr. 3
"Don't blame me." They point their crook-ed lit-tle fing-ers at ev-'ry-bod-y else.
Gtr. 1
choke
Gtr. 3
Gtr. 5
w/distortion
mf
P.M. throughout

G5
Spend all their time feel- in' sor - ry for them- selves. Vic - tim of this,
Gtr. 1
choke
Gtr. 1
Gtr. 2
Gtr. 3
Gtr. 5

A5
vic - tim of that, your ma - ma's too thin, and your dad - dy's too fat. Get o-
Background vocals: Get o -
mp
mf
end Rhy. Fig. 1

Chorus:
D5
F5
- ver it.
- ver it.
Get o - ver it.
Get o - ver it.
Gtr. 1
Lead Fig. 1A
Gtr. 4
w/slide
Rhy. Fig. 2
Gtr. 2
Rhy. Fig. 3
Gtr. 3

G5
All this whin-in' and cry-in' and pitch-in' a fit, get o-
get o-
T
A
B
15
(15)
13
15
(15)
T
A
B
12
(12)
10
12
(12)
T
A
B
3
3
3
5
5
5
5
5
5
T
A
B
10 10 12 13 10 12
8 8 8 8 8 8
12 12 14 15 12 14
10 10 10 10 10 10
12 12 14 12 12 12 12
10 10 10 10 10 10 10

D5
- ver it, get o - ver it.
- ver it, get o - ver it.
end Lead Fig. 1
1/2
end Lead Fig. 1A
end Rhy. Fig. 2
end Rhy. Fig. 3

Interlude:
Guitar Solo: (Glen Frey)
Gtr. 1
D5
F5
G5
gradual release
Gtr. 3
Gtr. 5
A.H.

D5
Verse:
(add Keyboard)
w/Rhy. Fig. 1, Simile (Gtr. 3)
D5
You say you have-'nt been the same since you
Rhy. Fig. 4
A.H.
Rhy. Fig. 5
had your lit - tle crash, but you might feel bet - ter if they gave you some cash. The
Gtr. 1
Gtr. 5

w/Fill 1

more I think a - bout it, old Bil - ly was right. Let's
Background vocals: Let's

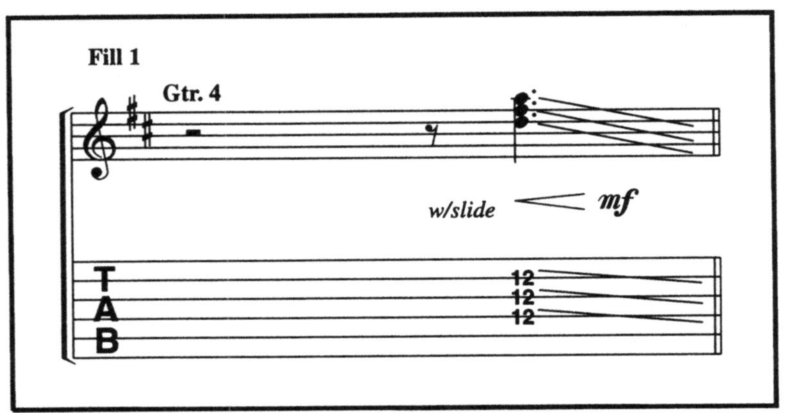

kill all the law - yers, kill em' to - night. You
kill all the law - yers, kill em' to - night.
Gtr. 2
T
A
B
7 7 7 7 7 7 (7 7) 5 5 5 5 7 7
15
0 0 2 3 0 2 0 (0) 0 2 0 3 0 2 5 5 5

G5
don't want to work; you want to live like a king but the
T
A
B
12
12
5
5
5
8
7

A5
big bad world does - n't owe you a thing.
Get o -
Background vocals: Get o -
end Rhy. Fig. 4
end Rhy. Fig. 5
Chorus:
with Lead Figs. 1 and 2 (Gtrs. 1 and 4) and Rhy. Fig. 2 (Gtr. 2)
D5
- ver it.
- ver it.
F5
Get o - ver it.
Get o - ver it.
Gtr. 5

To Coda
G5
If you don't want to play, then you might as well split. Get o-
Get o-
D5
- ver it, get o - ver it.
- ver it, get o - ver it.
Gtr. 5
Gtr. 6
w/slide
w/distortion
w/o slide
Interlude: w/Rhy. Fig. 3 (Gtr. 3)
Guitar Solo: (Joe Walsh)
Gtr. 5
D5 Rhy. Fig. 3A
F5
Gtr. 6

G5

D5
end Rhy. Fig. 3A

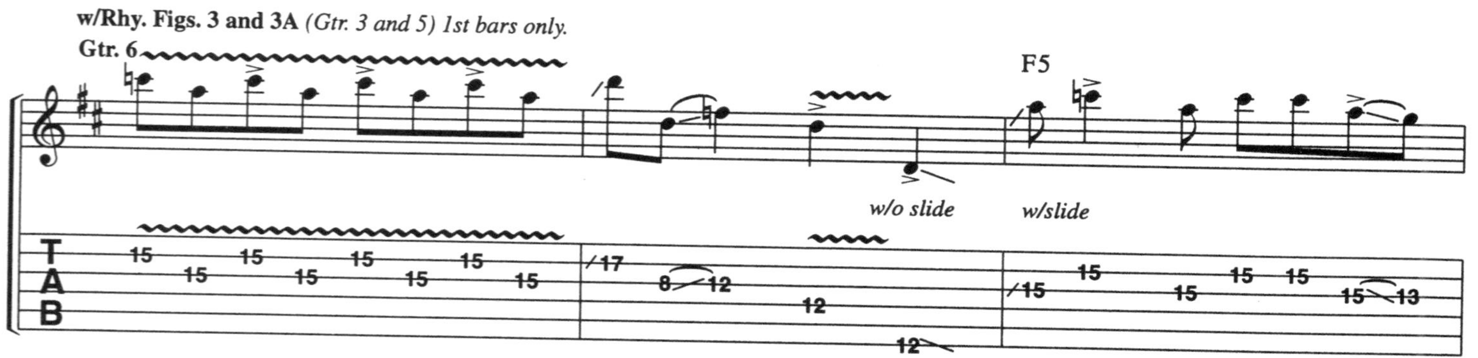
w/Rhy. Figs. 3 and 3A (Gtr. 3 and 5) 1st bars only.
Gtr. 6
F5
w/o slide
w/slide

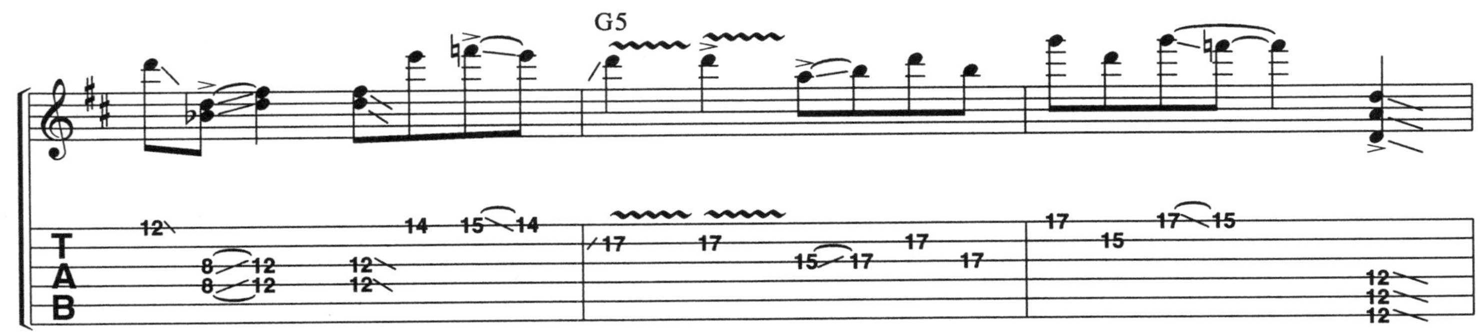

D5

It's like

Gtr. 3

Gtr. 5

Gtr. 6

*Gradual slide, begin here.

Bridge:
C
D
C
go-ing to con-fes-sion every time I hear you speak.
You're

C
A
mak- ing the most___ of your los - in' streak.
Some call it sick, but
T
A
B

I call it weak.
Yeah, yeah, yeah, yeah. You
mf

Verse:
w/Rhy. Figs. 3 and 4 (Gtrs. 1 and 5)
w/Rhy. Fig. 1, simile (Gtr. 3)
D5
w/Fill 1
drag it a - round_ like a ball and chain._ You wal- low in the guilt; you
w/Fill 1
wal- low in the pain. You wave it like a flag, you wear it like a crown. Got your
G5
mind in the gutt - er, bring- in' ev -'ry - bod - y down. Bitch a - bout the pres- ent, and
A5
blame it on the past. I'd like to find your inn - er child and kick it's lit - tle ass.___ Get o-
Background vocals: Get o -
Chorus:
w/Lead Figures 1 and 2 (Gtrs. 1 and 4) and Rhy. Fig. 2 (Gtr. 2)
w/Rhy. Fig. 2 (Gtr. 2) and Rhy. Figs. 3 and 3A (Gtrs. 3 and 5)
D5
F5
- ver it. Get o - ver it. All this
- ver it. Get o - ver it.
G5
D5
bitch- in' and moan- in' and pitch- in' a fit, get o - ver it, get o -
get o - ver it, get o -
w/Rhy. Figs. 3 and 3A, 1st 6 bars only (Gtrs. 3 and 5)
D
- ver it. Get o - ver it. Get o -
- ver it. Get o - ver it. Get o -
F
G
- ver it. It's got- ta stop some-time, so why don't you quit, get o-
- ver it. get o -

Outro:
w/Rhy. Figs. 3 and 3A (Gtrs. 3 and 5)
Guitar Solo: (Don Felder)
D
D5
- ver it, get o - ver it.
- ver it, get o - ver it.
Gtr. 3
Gtr. 2
Gtr. 5
Gtr. 7
w/distortion
F5

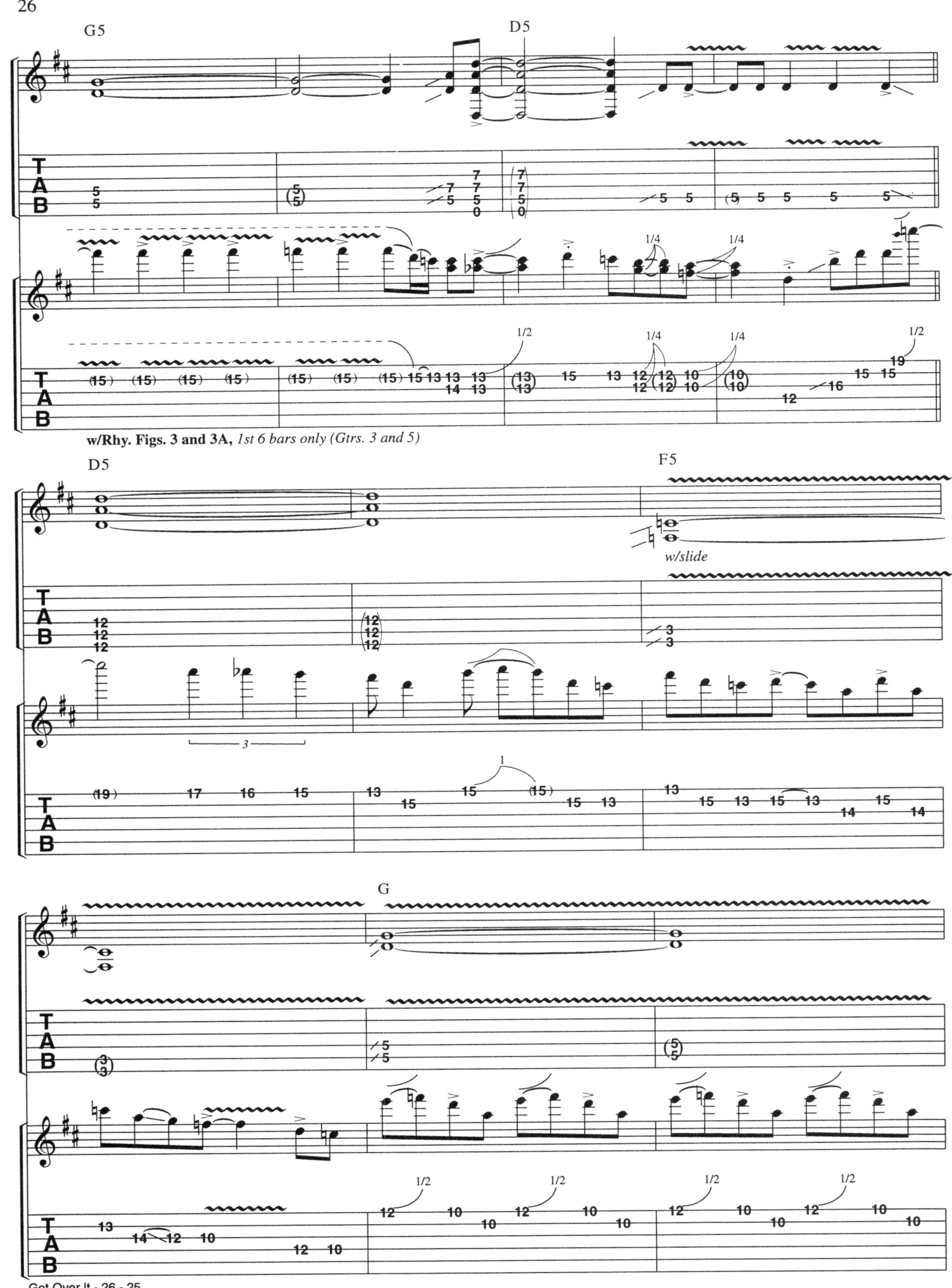
G5
D5
w/Rhy. Figs. 3 and 3A, 1st 6 bars only (Gtrs. 3 and 5)
D5
F5
w/slide
G

Freely
♩ = 112 approx.
D
ritard.
D5
Spoken: Get o-ver it!
Gtr. 2
Gtr. 3
Gtr. 5
Gtr. 7

# love will keep us alive

Words and Music by
JIM CAPALDI, PETER VALE and PAUL CARRACK

Esus

E

1. I___ was

Verse:
Asus2
F♯m7(4)
stand - ing,_ all a - lone___ a - gainst the world_ out - side.___
Gtr. 1

D6sus2
You were search - ing,
for a place to hide.
TAB
Esus
E
Asus2/E
Lost and lone - ly,
TAB
F♯m7(4)
now you've giv - en me the will to sur - vive.
TAB
D6sus2
When we're hun - gry,
TAB

Esus
E
Asus2
love will keep us a - live.
(2.) Don't you
Verse 2: (Kybd. enters:)
Asus2/E
F♯m7(4)
wor - ry
some- times you've just got- ta
let it ride.
D6sus2
The world is
chang - ing,
right be- fore your eyes.
Esus
E
Asus2
Now, I've found you;
TAB

F♯m7(4)
there's no more_ emp - ti - ness_____ in - side.__ When we're

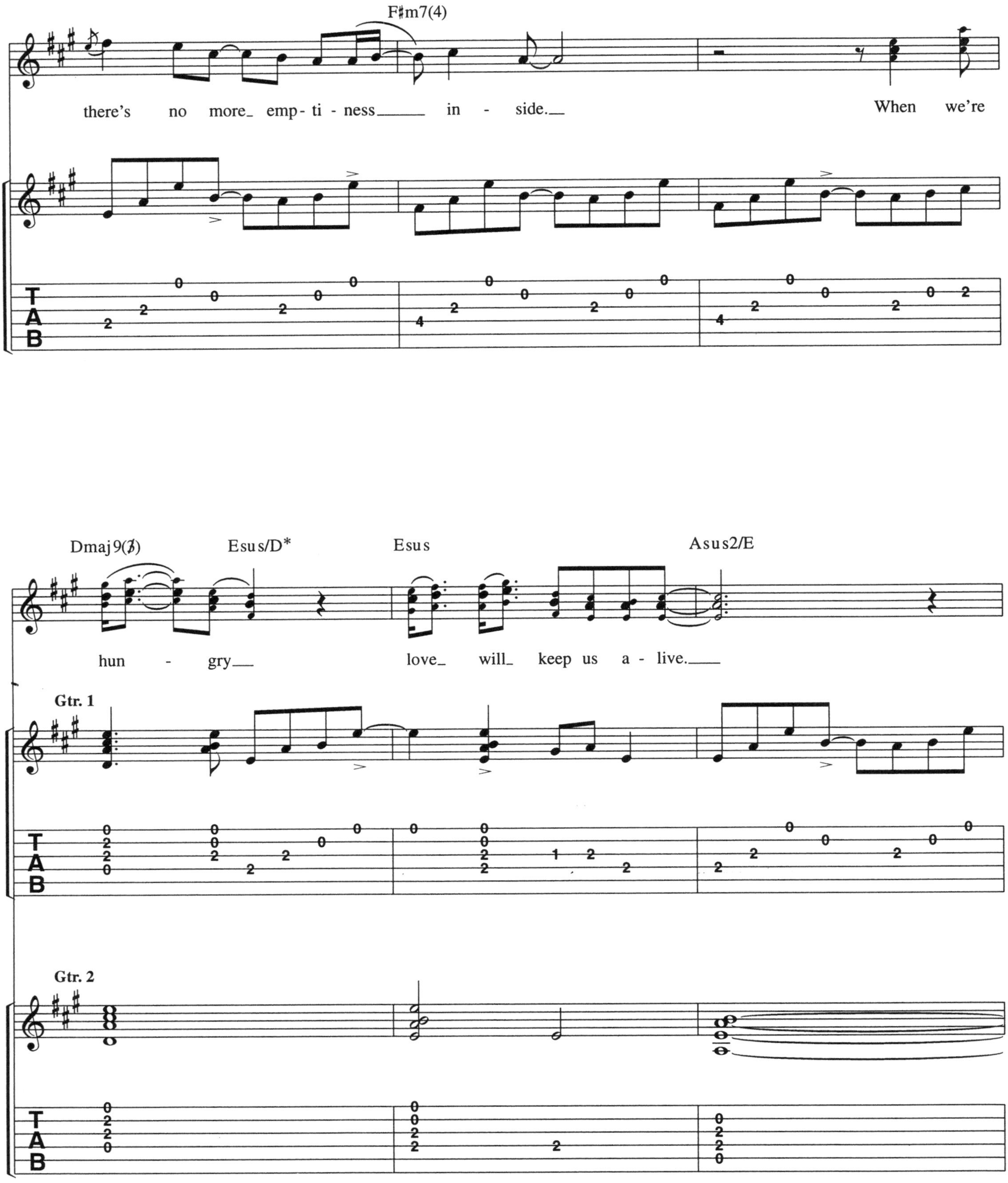

Dmaj9(3) Esus/D* Esus Asus2/E

hun - gry__ love_ will_ keep us a - live.____

**Gtr. 1**

**Gtr. 2**

*Bass Gtr. note.

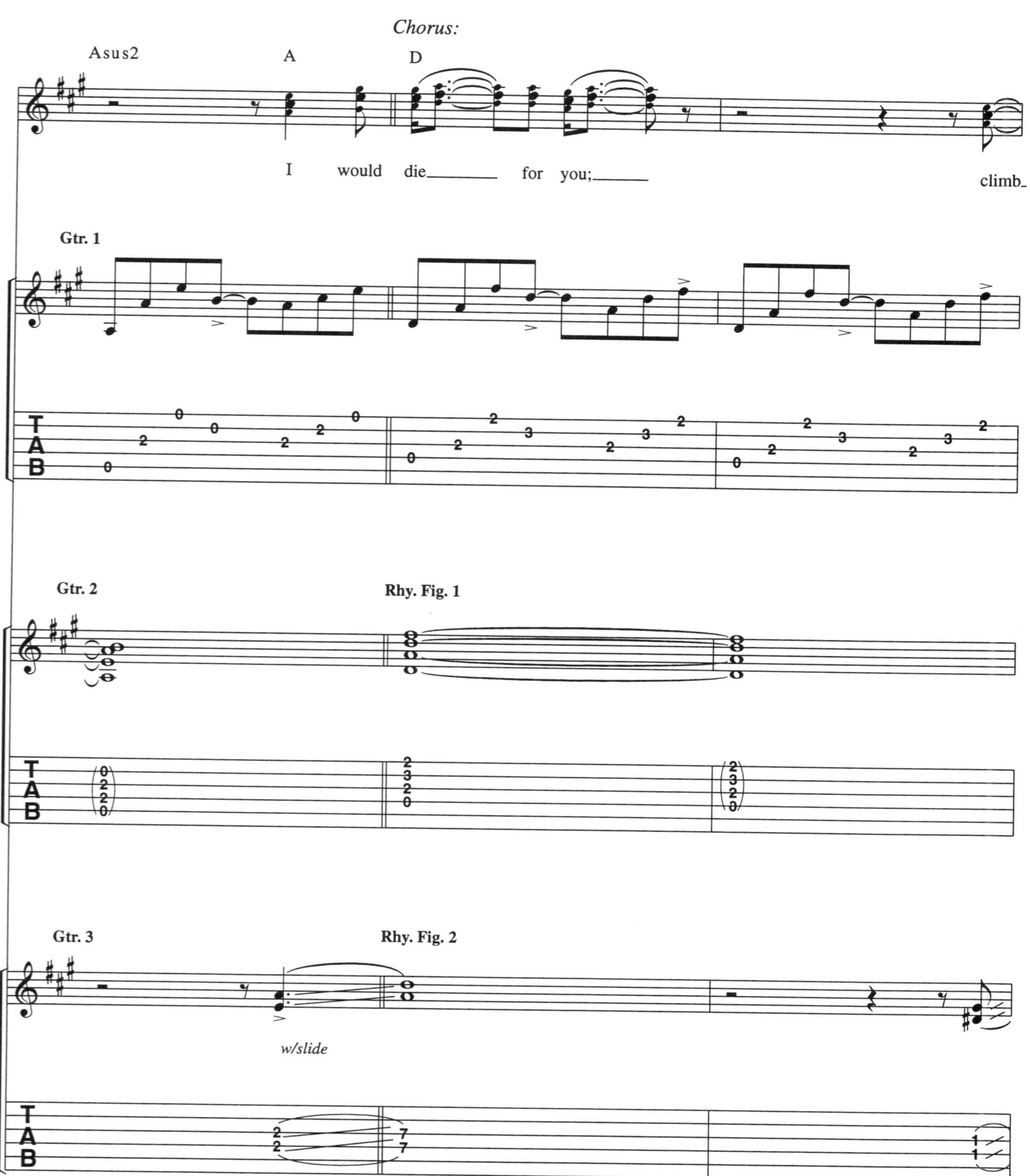
Chorus:
Asus2
A
D
I would die for you; climb
Gtr. 1
Gtr. 2
Rhy. Fig. 1
Gtr. 3
Rhy. Fig. 2
w/slide

F♯m
Bm7
— the high - est moun - tain.
Ba - by,
TAB
TAB
TAB

E
E/D
E/C♯
E/B
there's
noth- ing I
would- n't
do.
(3.) Now I've
end Rhy. Fig. 1
end Rhy. Fig. 2

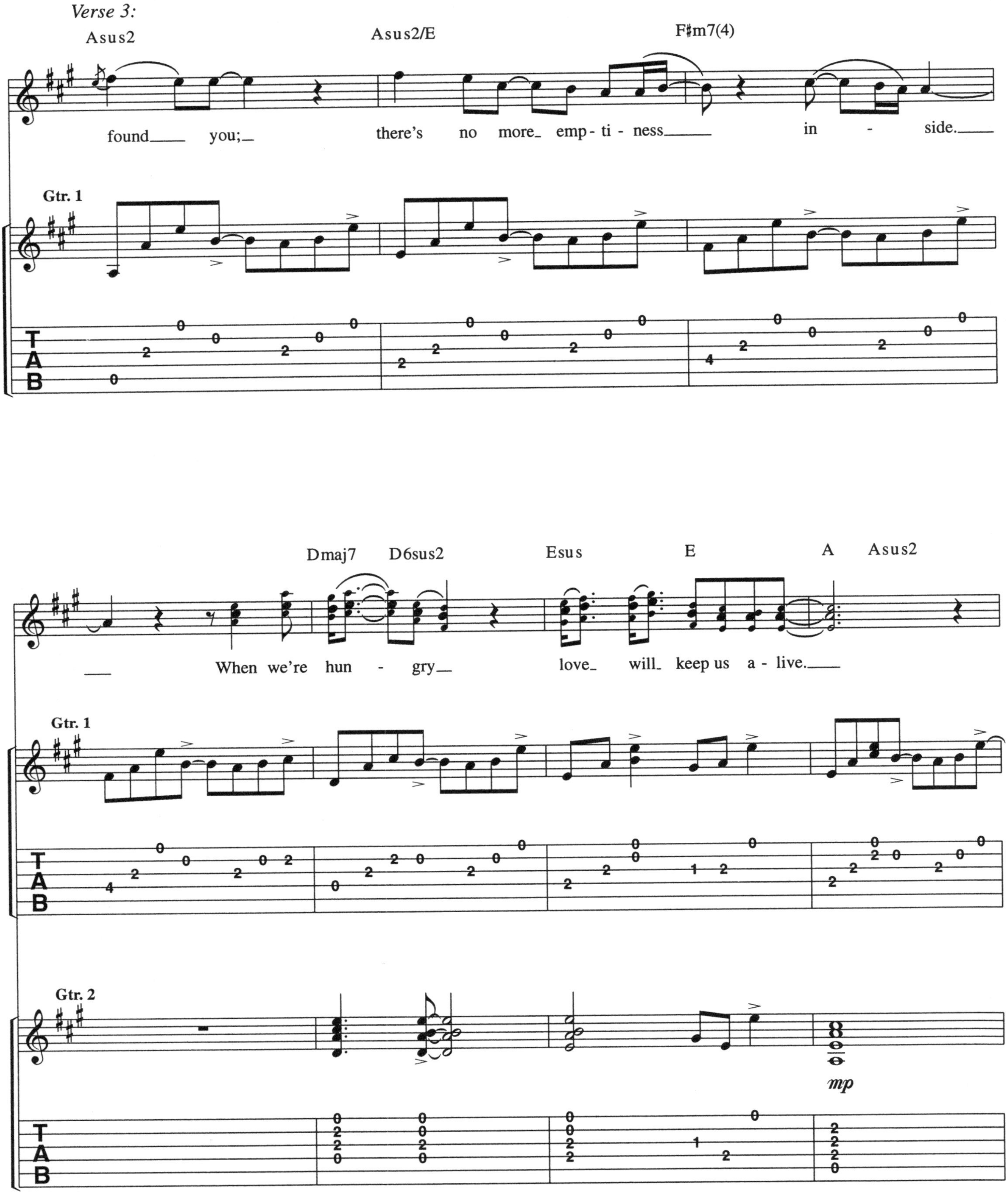

*Verse 3:*

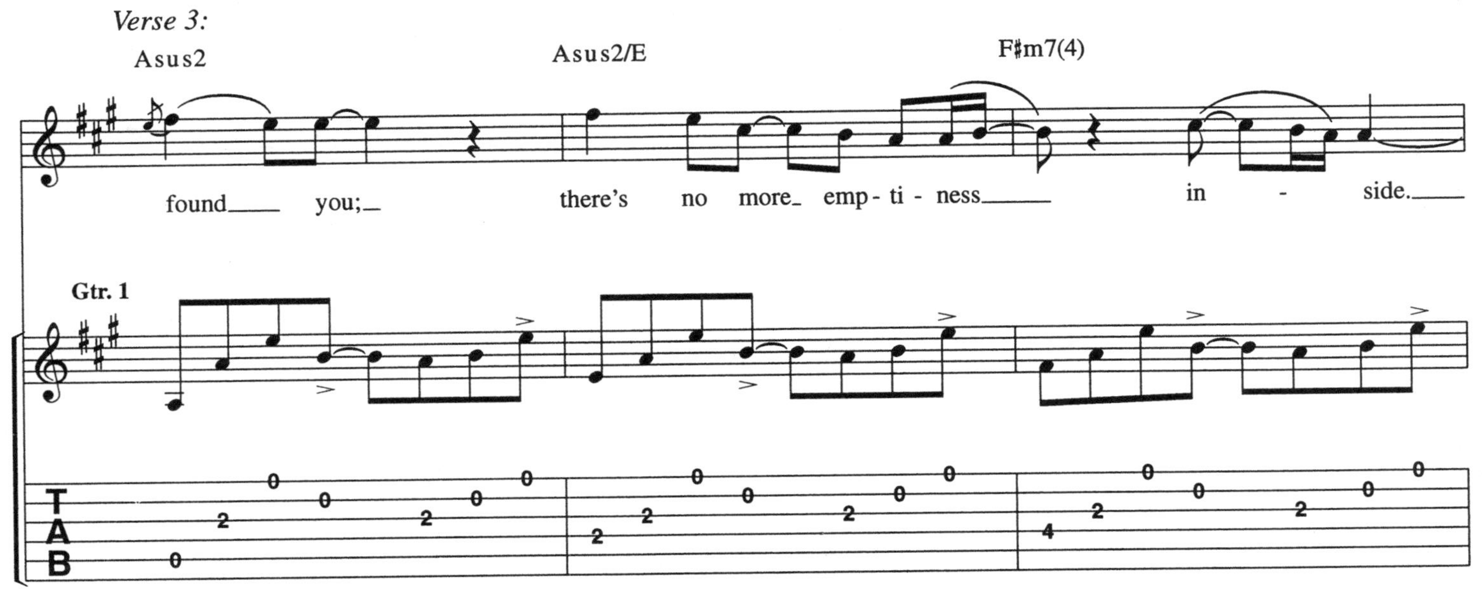
Asus2
Asus2/E
F♯m7(4)
found you; there's no more emp-ti-ness in-side.
Gtr. 1
T
A
B

Dmaj7 D6sus2 Esus E A Asus2

When we're hun - gry love will keep us a - live.

Gtr. 1

Gtr. 2

*mp*

Guitar Solo:
Asus2/E
Gtr. 1
Gtr. 2
Gtr. 3
f w/slide
F♯m7(4)
D6sus2

Asus2
A
I would

Chorus:
w/Rhy. Figs. 1 & 2
D
F♯m
die for you; climb the high - est moun -
Gtr. 1
Bm7
- tain. Ba - by, there's noth - ing I would - n't
E
E/D
E/C♯
end Rhy. Figs. 1 & 2
E/B
Verse 4:
Asus2
do. (4.) I was stand - ing
Asus2/E
F♯m7(4)
all a - lone a - gainst the world out - side. You were

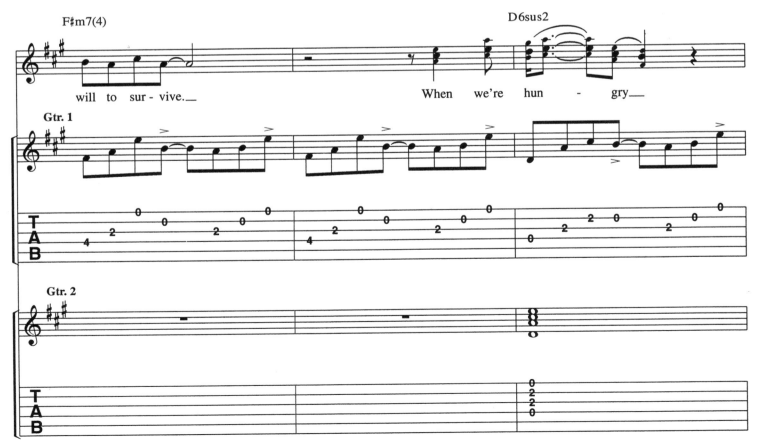

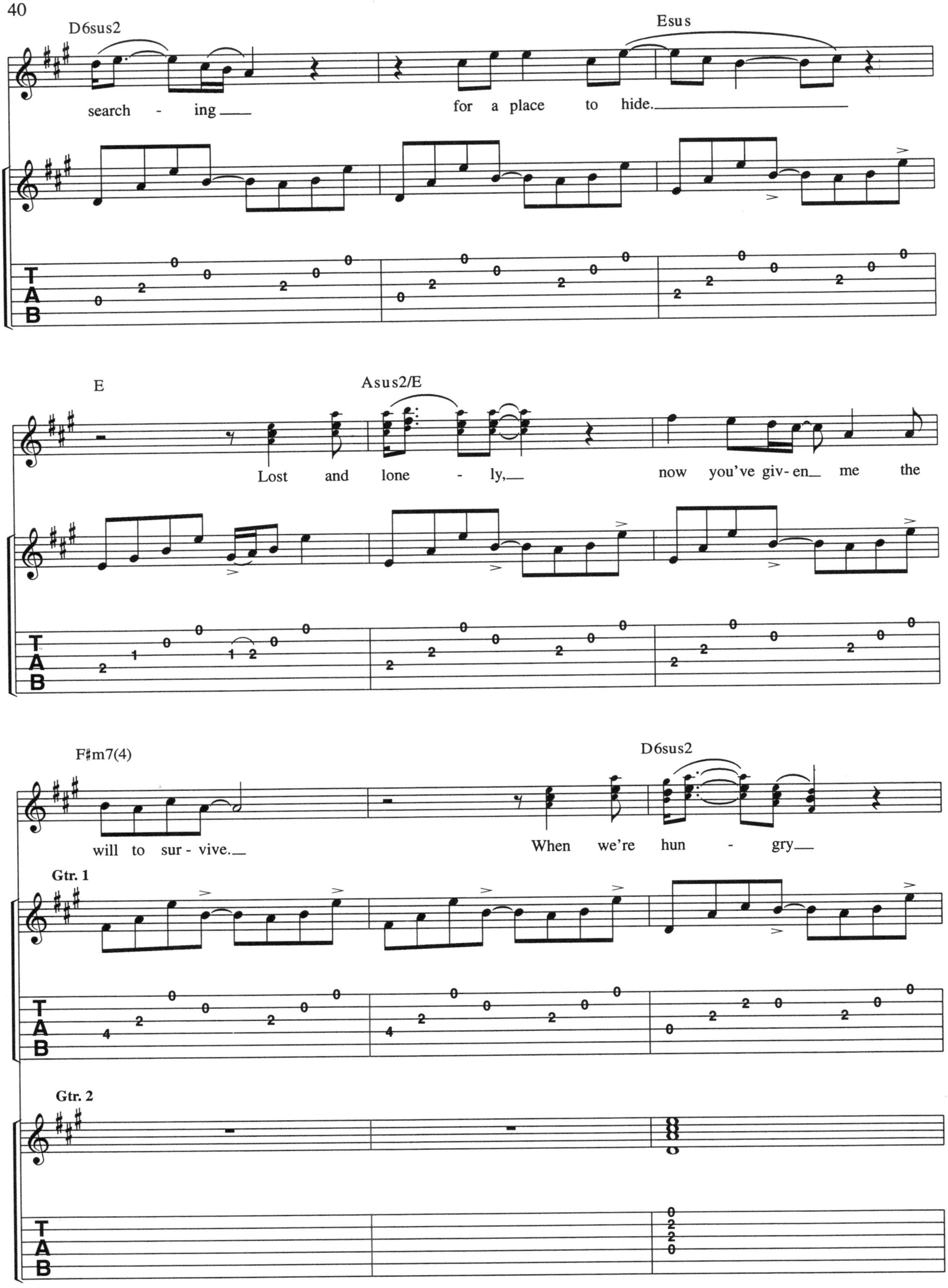

F♯m7(4)

D6sus2

will to sur - vive.___ When we're hun - gry___

Gtr. 1

TAB

Gtr. 2

TAB

Esus
Asus2/E
F♯m7(4)
love_ will_ keep us a - live.
When we're
Gtr. 1
Gtr. 2
Gtr. 3

Gtr. 2 continues simile:
D6sus2
Esus
E
Asus2/E
hun - gry
love will keep us a - live.
Gtr. 1
Gtr. 3
F♯m7(4)
D6sus2
Esus
When we're hun - gry
love will keep us a - live.
Gtr. 1
Gtr. 2
Gtr. 3

Asus2
ritard.
T
A
B

# the girl from yesterday

Words and Music by
GLENN FREY and JACK TEMPCHIN

G
G7
C
D
Gtype2
D7
Ctype2
D/F♯
A/E
Em7
Em
G/B
Am7
A7sus
D7sus
Bm7
Dsus2
D5
E

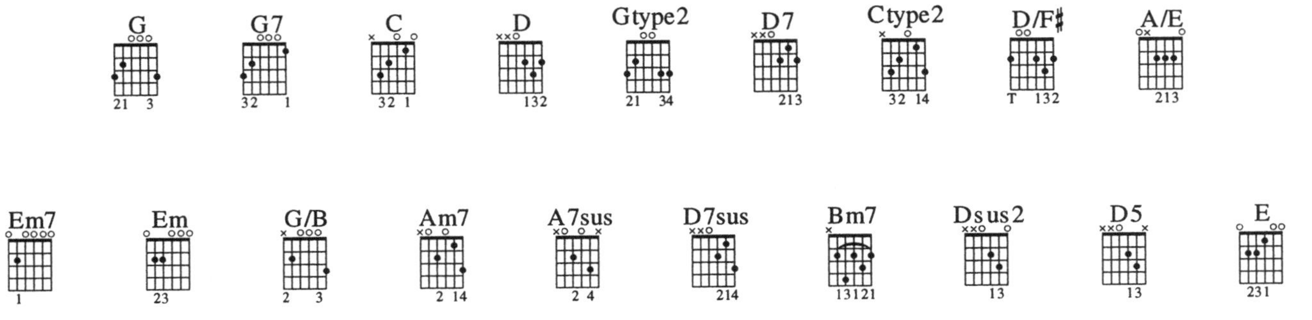

**Moderate country ballad** ♩ = 100

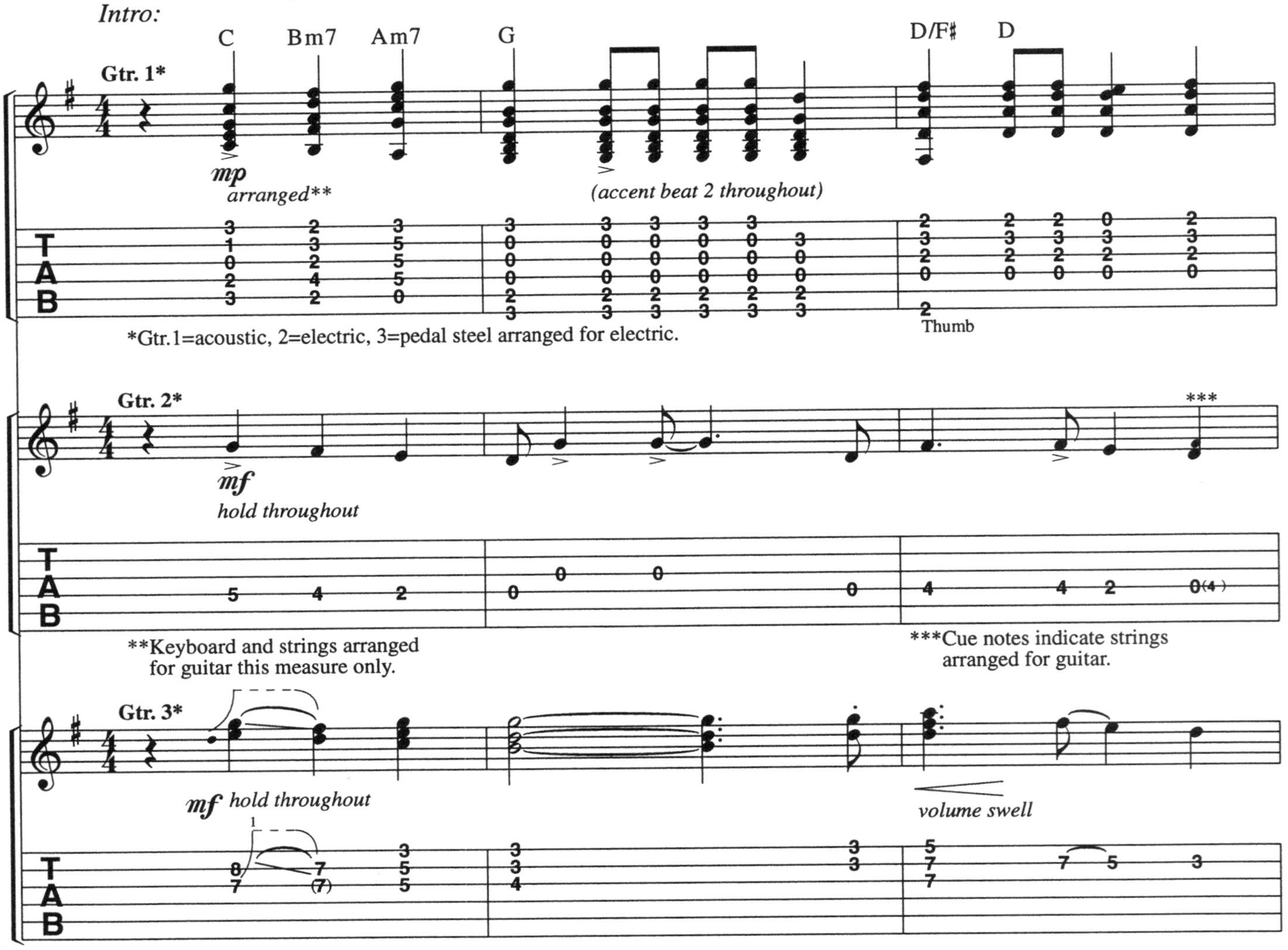

Intro:
C
Bm7
Am7
G
D/F♯
D
Gtr. 1*
mp
arranged**
(accent beat 2 throughout)
Thumb
*Gtr.1=acoustic, 2=electric, 3=pedal steel arranged for electric.
Gtr. 2*
mf
hold throughout
**Keyboard and strings arranged
for guitar this measure only.
***Cue notes indicate strings
arranged for guitar.
Gtr. 3*
mf hold throughout
volume swell

Verse:
G
D/F♯ D D7
Gtr. 1 G
G7
It was-n't real - ly sad___ the way they said_
mp
sideways vibrato
C
D
___ good - by.__
Or may-be it__ just_ hurt___ so bad___ she

G(type2)
D
G(type2)
could - n't cry.
He packed his things, walked
Gtr. 3
hold
Gtr. 3
G 7
C
out the door and drove a - way, and
Gtr. 2
Gtr. 3
gradual bend
1/2
*Use fingers 2 and 3 to bend the third string.

G(type2)
D
G
D
she be - came the girl from yes - ter - day.
He
mp
*Resolve to fourth fret third string next measure and sustain.
choke
harm.
Verse:
Gtrs.1, 2 and 3 continue simile:
G
G7
C
took a plane a - cross the sea to some for - eign land.
She
D
D7
G
stayed at home and tried so hard to un - der - stand,
D
G
G7
how some - one who had been so close could
C
C(type2)
C
G
be so far a - way, and she be - came the

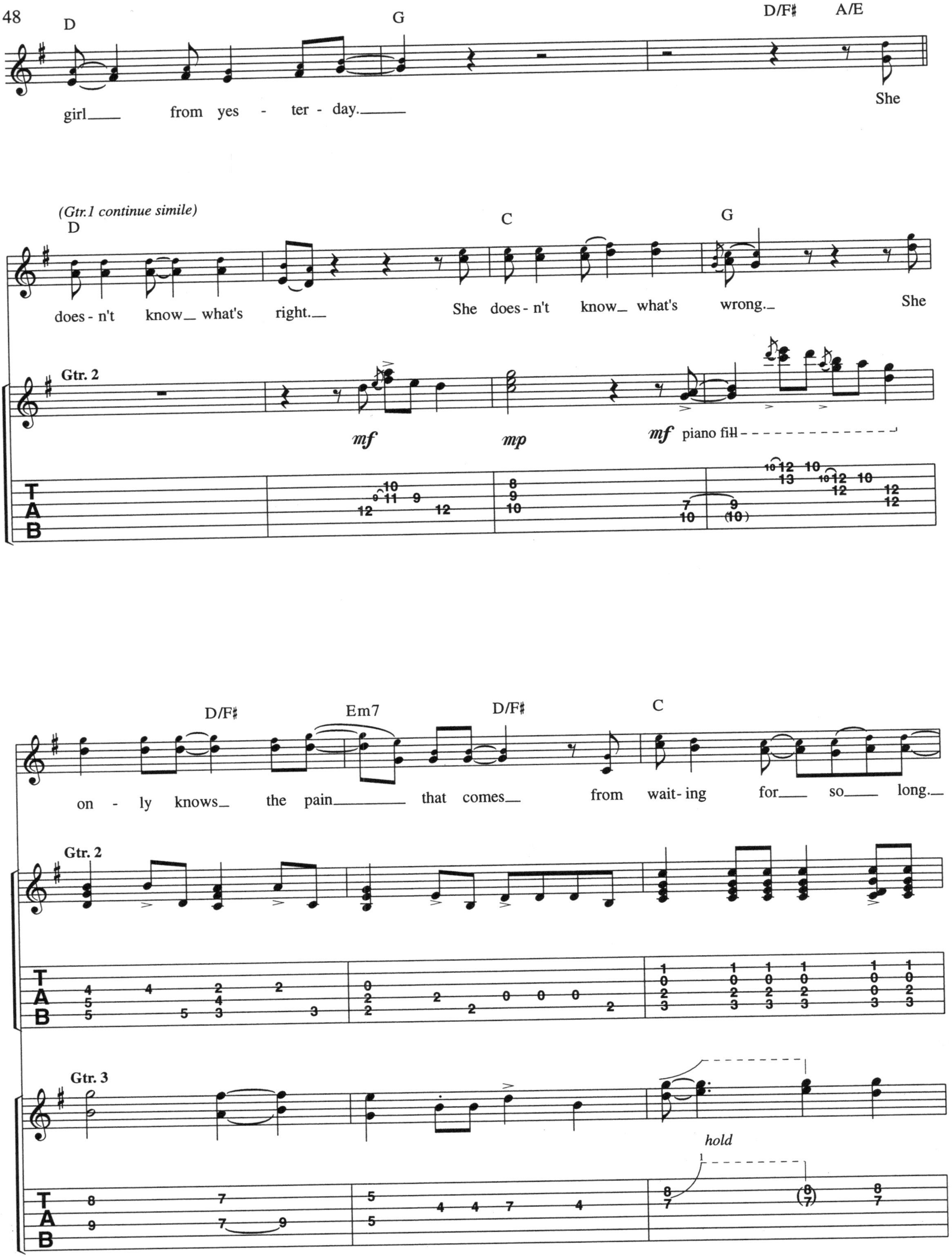

D/F♯ Em7 D/F♯ C

on - ly knows_ the pain___ that comes_ from wait - ing for_ so_ long._

Gtr. 2

Gtr. 3

hold

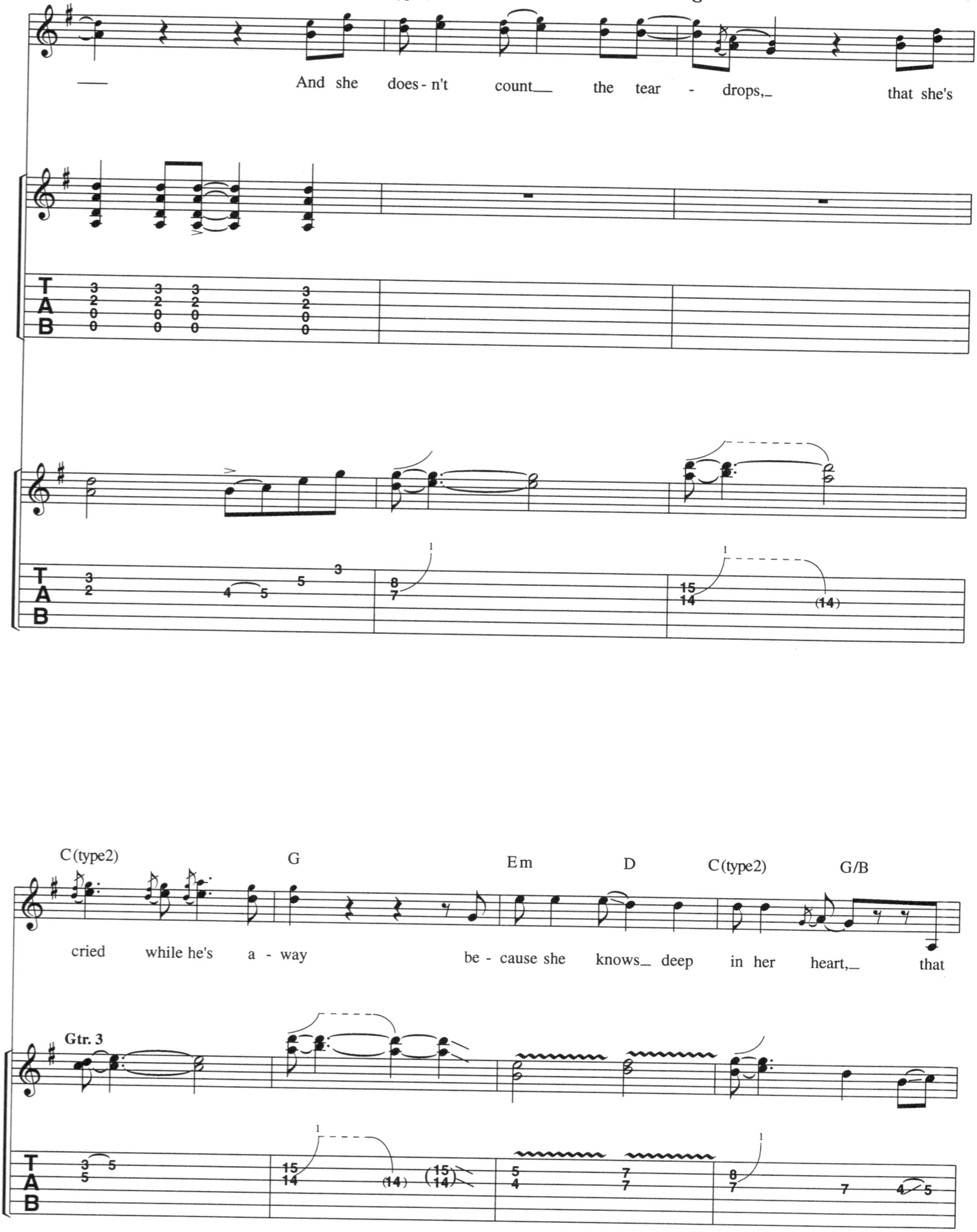

D C(type2) G

And she does-n't count the tear-drops, that she's

Gtr. 3

C(type2)
G
Em
D
C(type2)
G/B
cried while he's a-way
be-cause she knows deep in her heart, that
Gtr. 3

Am7
A7sus
D7sus
D
he'll be back some - day.
f
Guitar Solo:
Gtr.3 continues simile:
G
G7
C
Bm7
Am7
Gtr. 1
Gtr. 2
G
D
Dsus2
D5
G
G(type2)
E
The
mf
*Pull-off from third fret second string to first fret.

Verse:
A
A 7
D
light's on in the win - dow; she's waiting by the phone,
Gtr. 1
D5
E
talk-ing to a mem-o - ry, that's
A
E
(A/C♯ E 7/B)*
A
nev - er com-ing home. She dreams of his re - turn -
*Passing chords in parenthesis-optional throughout: not played by Gtr.1 originally.
A 7
D
D5
(C♯m/A B m/A)
- ing, and the things that he might say. But she'll

A
E
A
(B m/A C♯m/A)
al - ways be___ the girl from yes - ter - day.___
TAB

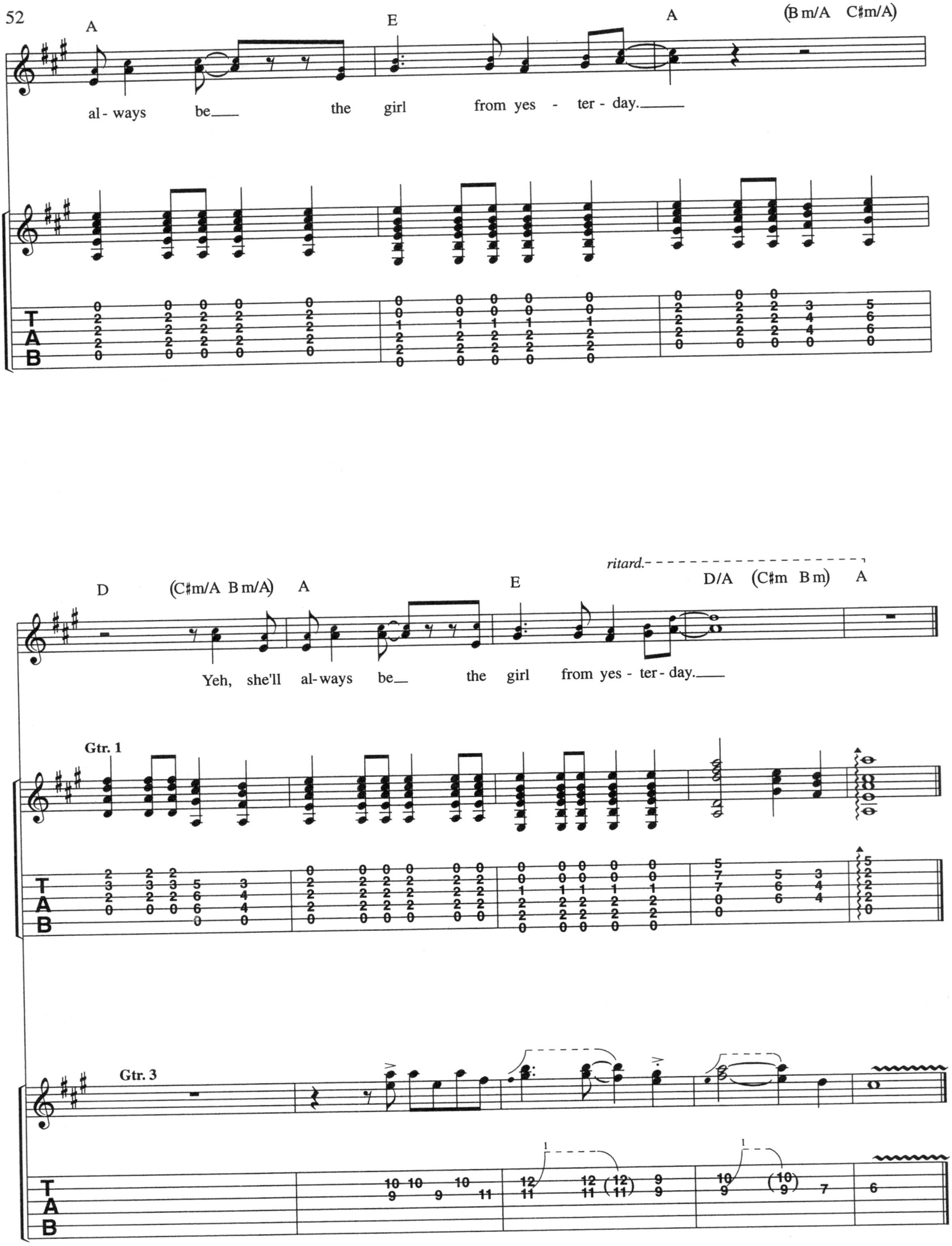

ritard.

D (C♯m/A B m/A) A E D/A (C♯m B m) A

Yeh, she'll al - ways be__ the girl from yes - ter - day.___

Gtr. 1

TAB

Gtr. 3

TAB

# pretty maids all in a row

Words and Music by
JOE WALSH and JOE VITALE

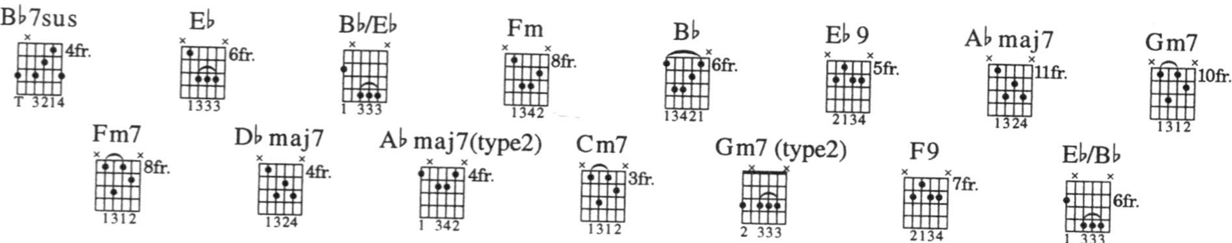


**Moderately slow ♩ = 96**
**Triplet feel (♫ = ♩♪ triplet)**
*Intro:*

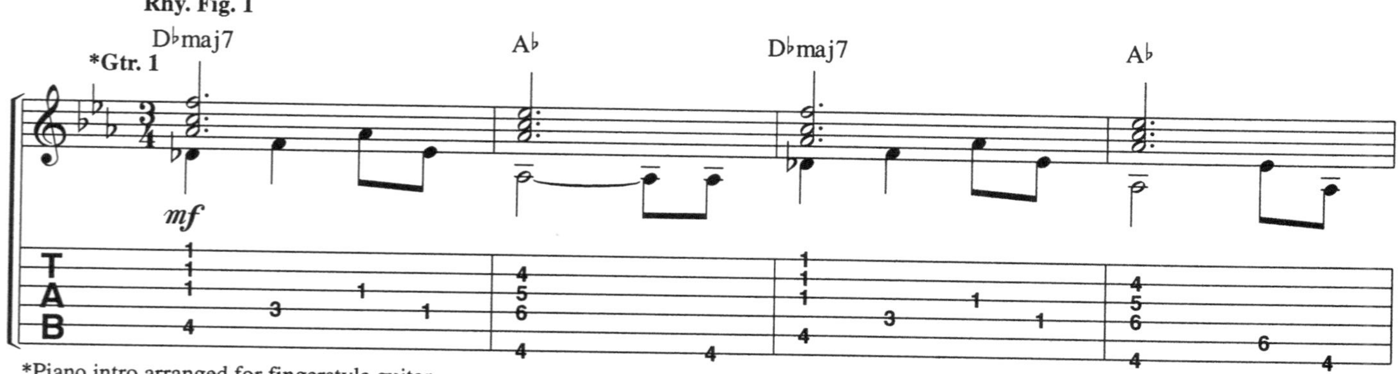


*Piano intro arranged for fingerstyle guitar.

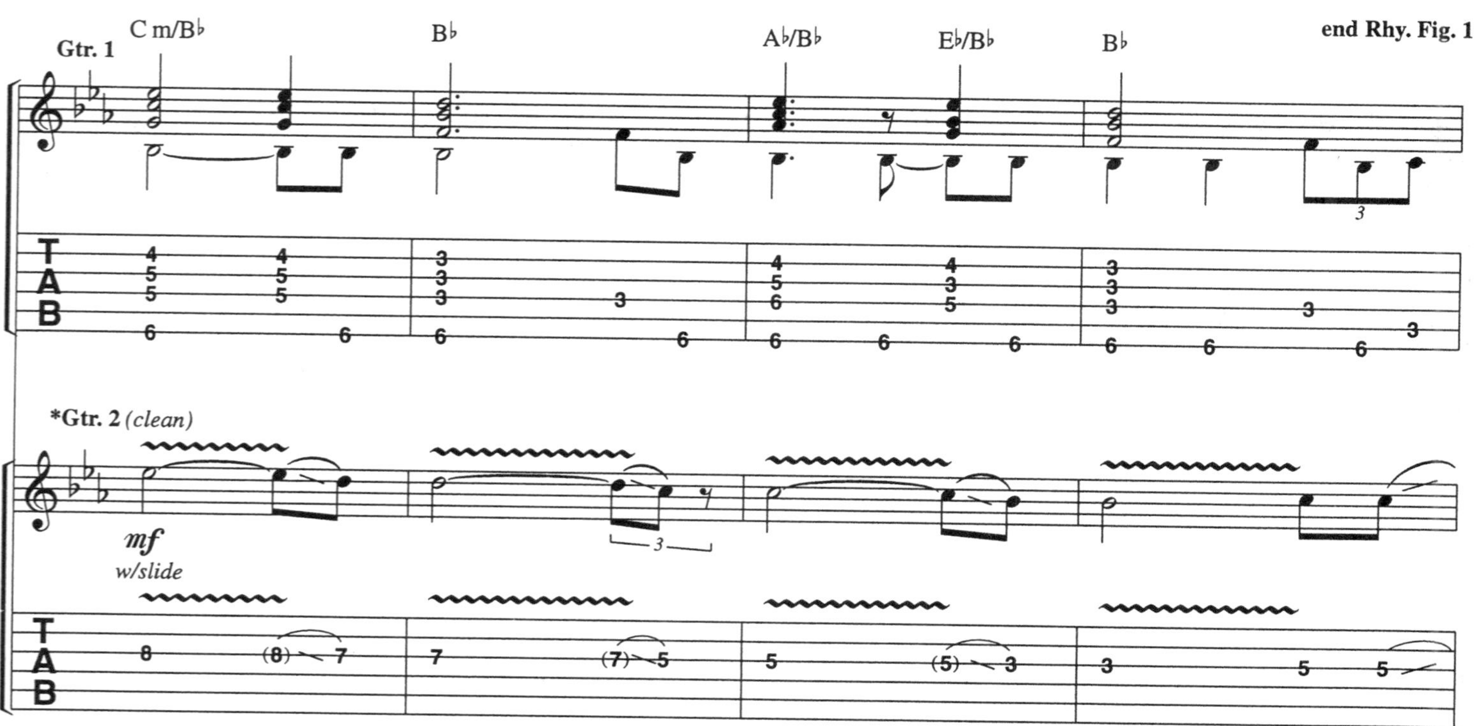


*12-string electric.

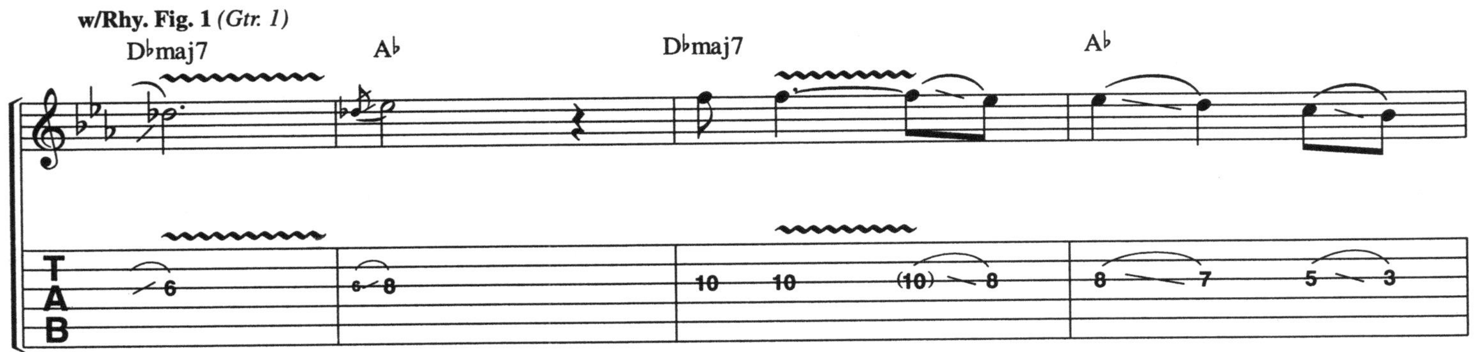

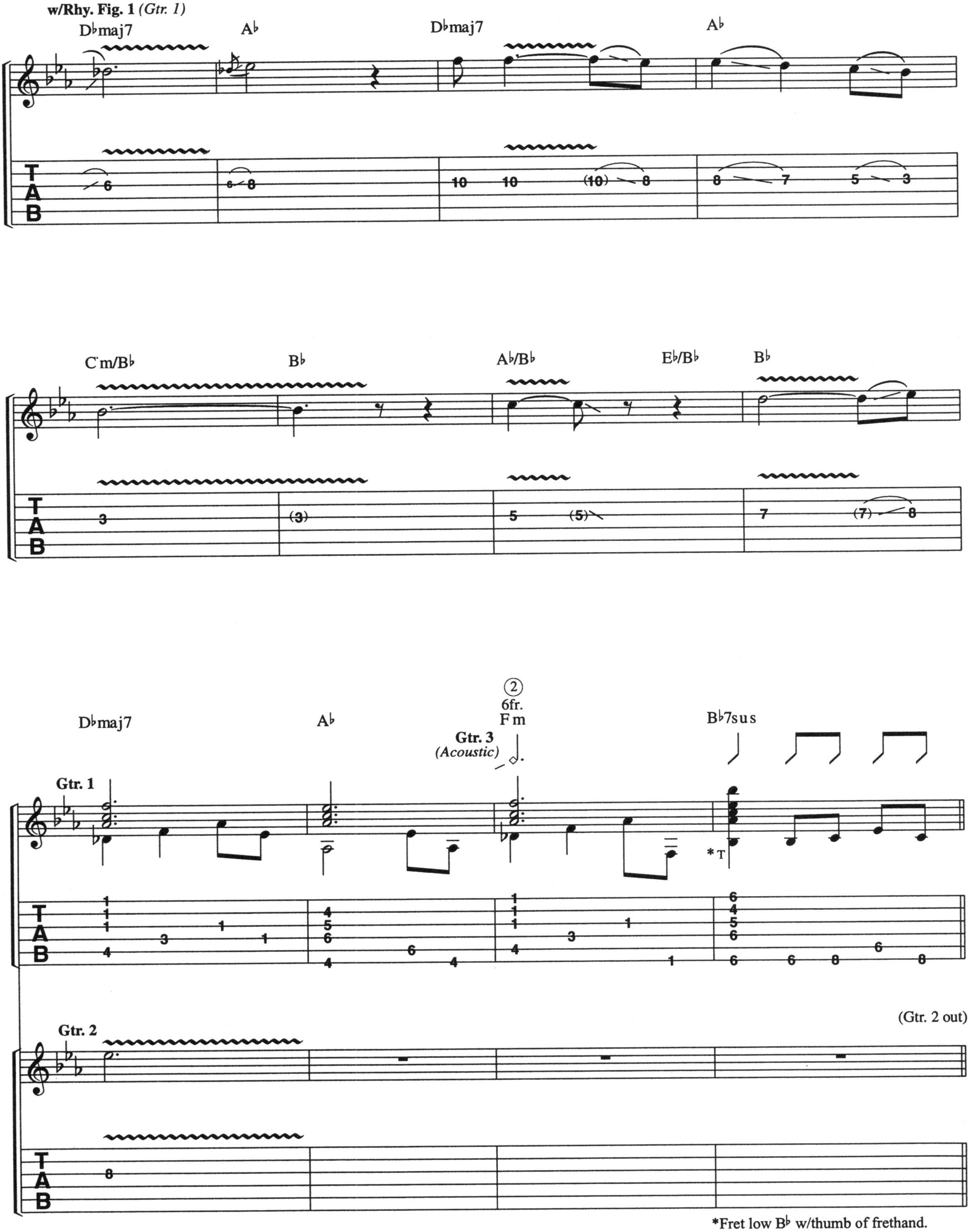

D♭maj7 A♭ Fm (6fr.) B♭7sus

Gtr. 3 (Acoustic)

Gtr. 1

Gtr. 2

(Gtr. 2 out)

*Fret low B♭ w/thumb of frethand.

*Verse:*

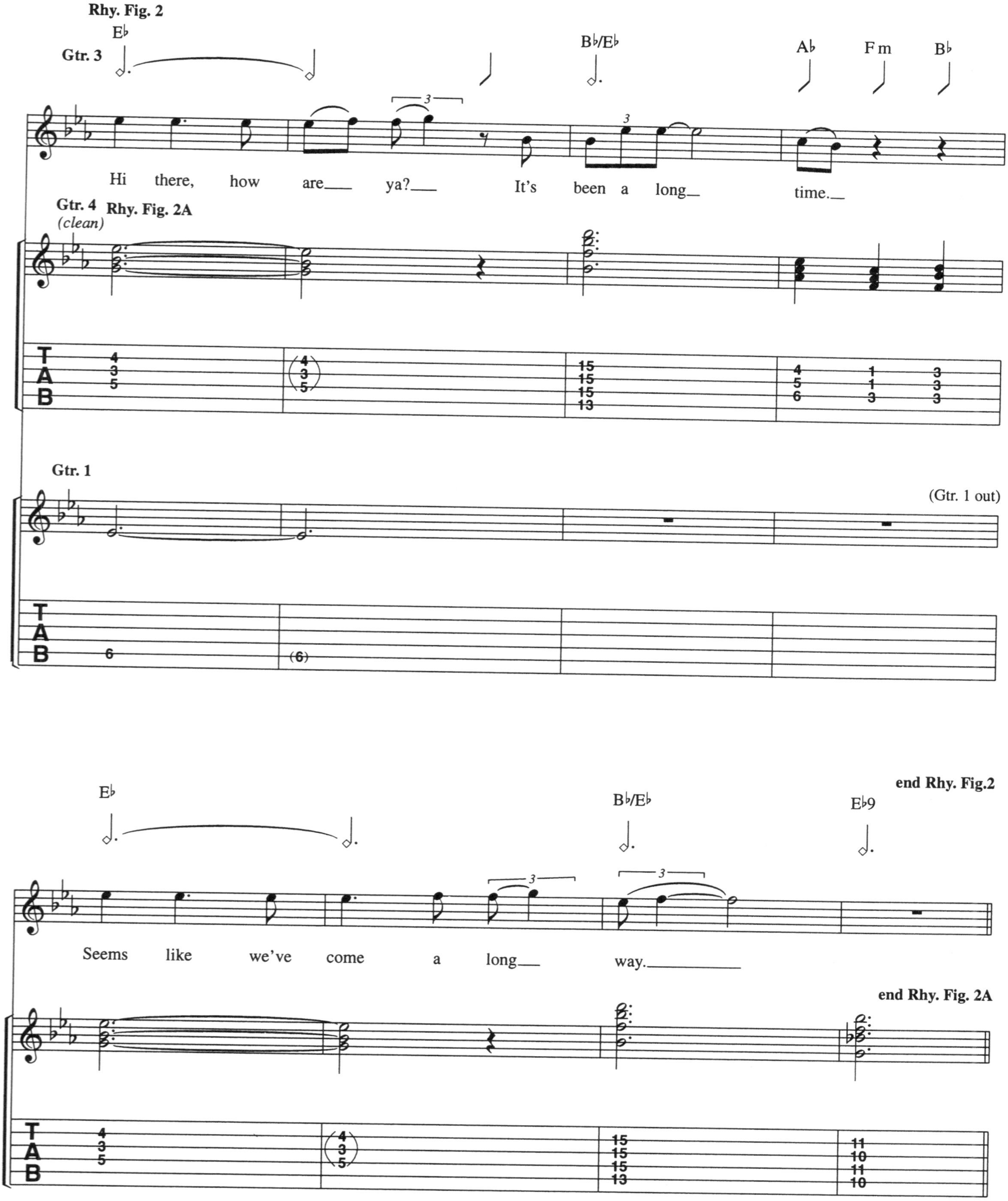

Rhy. Fig. 2
E♭
Gtr. 3
B♭/E♭
A♭
F m
B♭
Hi there, how are___ ya?___ It's been a long___ time.___
Gtr. 4 Rhy. Fig. 2A
(clean)
Gtr. 1
(Gtr. 1 out)
E♭
B♭/E♭
E♭9
end Rhy. Fig.2
Seems like we've come a long___ way.___
end Rhy. Fig. 2A

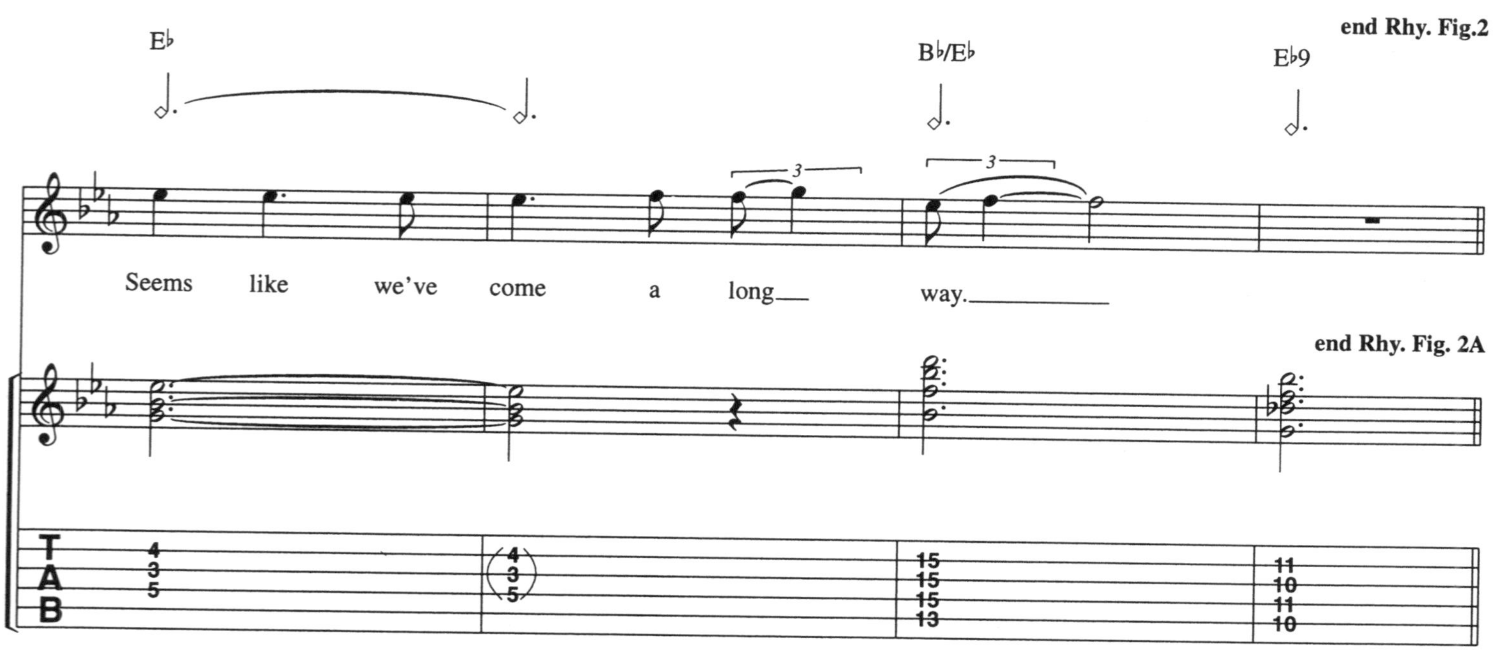

Bridges 1 & 2:
Rhy. Fig. 3
A♭maj7
Gm7
Fm7
N.C.
end Rhy. Fig. 3
1. My, but we learn so slow. And
2. (See additional lyrics)
Rhy. Fig. 3A
end Rhy. Fig 3A
w/Rhy. Figs. 3 & 3A (Gtrs. 3 and 4)
To Coda
he - ros, they come and they go and
Gtr. 3
D♭maj7
A♭maj7(type2)
leave us be - hind, as if we 'sposed to know.
Gtr. 4
Cm7
Gm7(type2)
why.
(why. )
Oh tell me

E♭
F9
E♭/B♭
B♭
Why? Why do we
hold
hold
hold
T
A
B

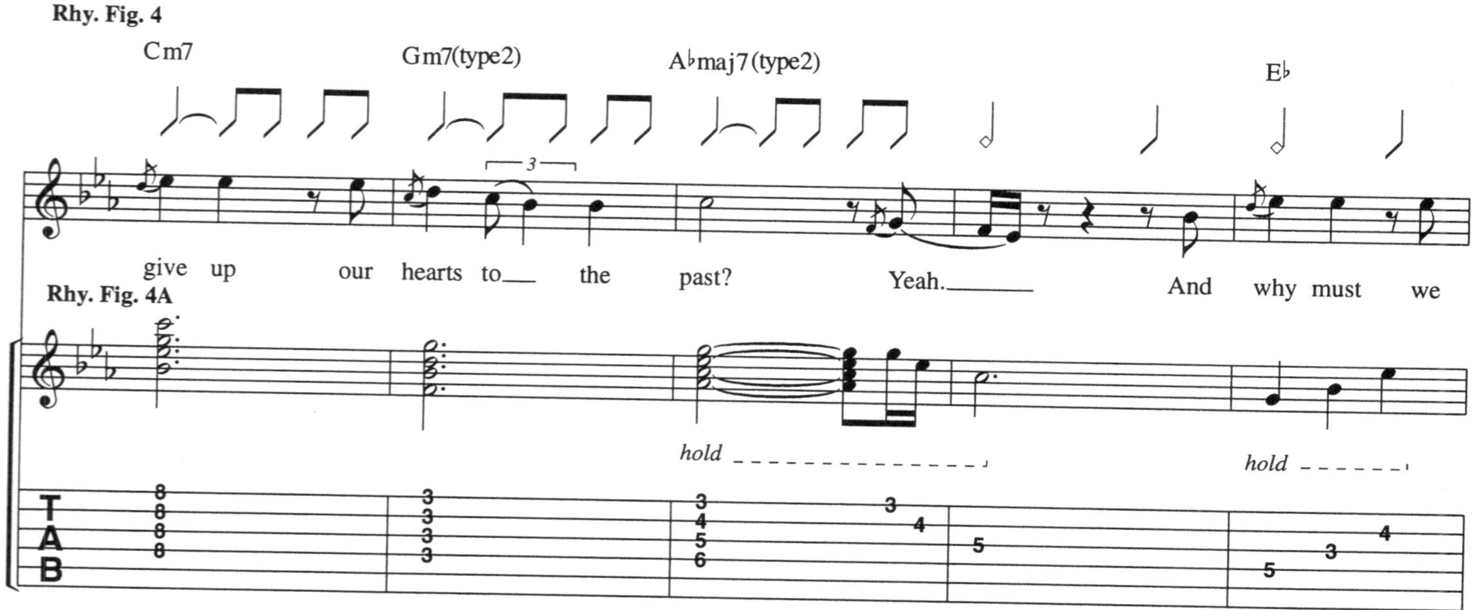
Rhy. Fig. 4
Cm7
Gm7(type2)
A♭maj7(type2)
E♭
give up our hearts to the past? Yeah. And why must we
Rhy. Fig. 4A
hold
hold
T
A
B

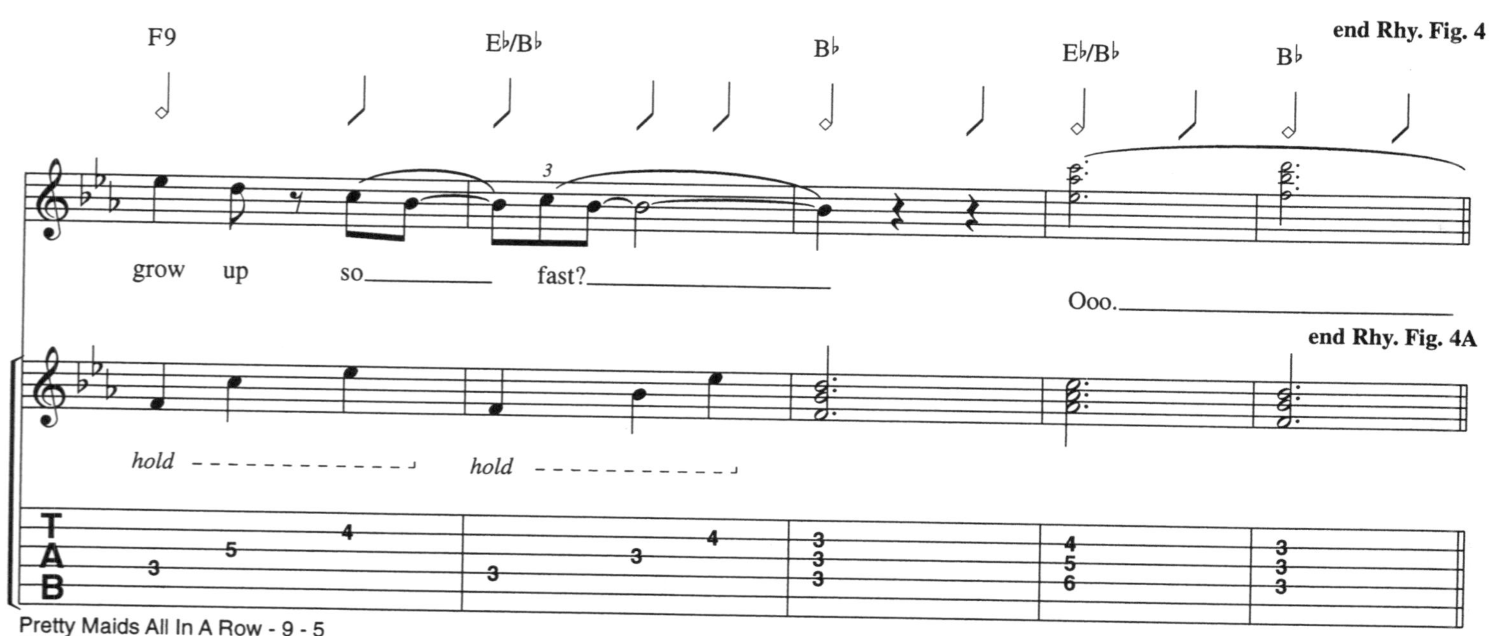
F9
E♭/B♭
B♭
E♭/B♭
B♭
end Rhy. Fig. 4
grow up so fast?
Ooo.
end Rhy. Fig. 4A
hold
hold
T
A
B

Guitar Solo:
w/Rhy. Figs. 2 & 2A (Gtrs. 3 and 4)
E♭
B♭/E♭
A♭
Fm
B♭
Gtr. 2
w/slide
hold
E♭
B♭/E♭
E♭9
D.S. al Coda
And all you
(Gtr. 2 out)
Coda
Cm7
Gm7(type2)
Fm7
B♭
E♭
B♭
Gtr. 3
love from a friend, it's nice to hear from you a - gain. And the
Gtr. 4
Chorus:
w/Rhy. Figs. 4&4A simile (1st 8 bars only), (Gtrs. 3 and 4) (2 times)
Cm7
Gm7
A♭maj7
stor - y - book comes to a close.

E♭
F9
E♭/B♭
B♭
Gone are the rib - bons and bows.
Cm7
Gm7
A♭maj7
Things to re - mem - ber, and plac - es to go.
E♭
F9
E♭/B♭
B♭
Pret - ty maids all in a row. All in a
Outro:
w/Rhy. Figs. 4&4A simile (1st 8 bars only), (Gtrs. 3 and 4) (3 times)
Cm7
Gm7
A♭maj7
row.
(Ooo. )
Gtr. 2
w/slide
13 11
E♭
F9
E♭/B♭
All in a
(Ooo. )
8
(8)
Cm7
Gm7
A♭maj7
row.
(Ooo. )
(Ooo. )
6 8

E♭
F9
E♭/B♭
B♭
Ooo.
(Ooo.
Ooo.
)
Cm7
Gm7
A♭maj7
Ooo.
(Ooo.
Ooo.
)
E♭
F9
E♭/B♭
B♭
Ooo.
(Ooo.
Ooo.
)
w/Rhy. Figs. 4 & 4A simile (Gtrs. 3 and 4)
Cm7
Gm7
A♭maj7
Ooo.
(Ooo.
Ooo.
)
steady gliss.
T
A
B

*Bridge 2:*

And all you wishin' well fools with your fortunes,
Someone should send you a rose.
With love from a friend,
It's nice to hear from you again.

# learn to be still

Words and Music by
DON HENLEY and STAN LYNCH

C♯
F♯
B
D♯m7
bed.
You'd give anything to silence
those voic-es ring-ing in your
C♯
D♯m
B
head.
You thought you could find
hap-pi-ness
hold
D♯m7
B
D♯m7
just o-ver that green hill.
You thought you would be
A♯m7
B
1.
C♯
Gtr. 1
sat-is-fied,
but you nev-er will...
Learn to be still.

Continue rhy. simile
w/Fill 1 (Gtr. 4)
F♯
B
F♯
B
2.
C♯
Gtr. 1
Gtr. 1
well. Learn to be still.
Rhy. Fig. 1
Gtr. 3
mf
end Rhy. Fig. 1
Rhy. Fig. 1A
Gtr. 2
hold
end Rhy. Fig. 1A
Chorus:
w/Rhy. Figs. 1 (Gtr. 3) & 1A (Gtr. 2)
Learn to be still.
To Coda
You just keep on
(Last time)
Fill 1
Gtr. 4
mf

*Bridge:*

C♯ Gtr. 1 B

Now the flow- ers in your gar - den, they don't smell so

Gtr. 3

P.M.

Gtr. 2

*hold* *hold*

sweet, so sweet.

C♯

May- be you've for- got - en

P.M. P.M.

*hold*

D♯m7 C♯

the heav- en ly- ing at your feet. Hey, hey, yeah.

Gtr. 4

P.M.

TAB

hold

TAB

*Guitar Solo:*

F♯ *Continue rhy. simile* B

TAB

hold hold

TAB

*Verse 2:*
We are like sheep without a shepherd.
We don't know how to be alone.
So we wander 'round this desert
And wind up following the wrong gods home.
But the flock cries out for another
And they keep answering that bell.
And one more starry-eyed messiah
Meets a violent farewell...
*(To Chorus:)*

*Verse 3:*
There are so many contradictions
In all these messages we send.
We keep asking, "How do I get out of here?
Where do I fit in?"
Though the world is torn and shaken.
Even if your heart is breakin',
It's waiting for you to awaken
And someday you will...
*(To Chorus:)*

# tequila sunrise

Words and Music by
DON HENLEY and GLENN FREY

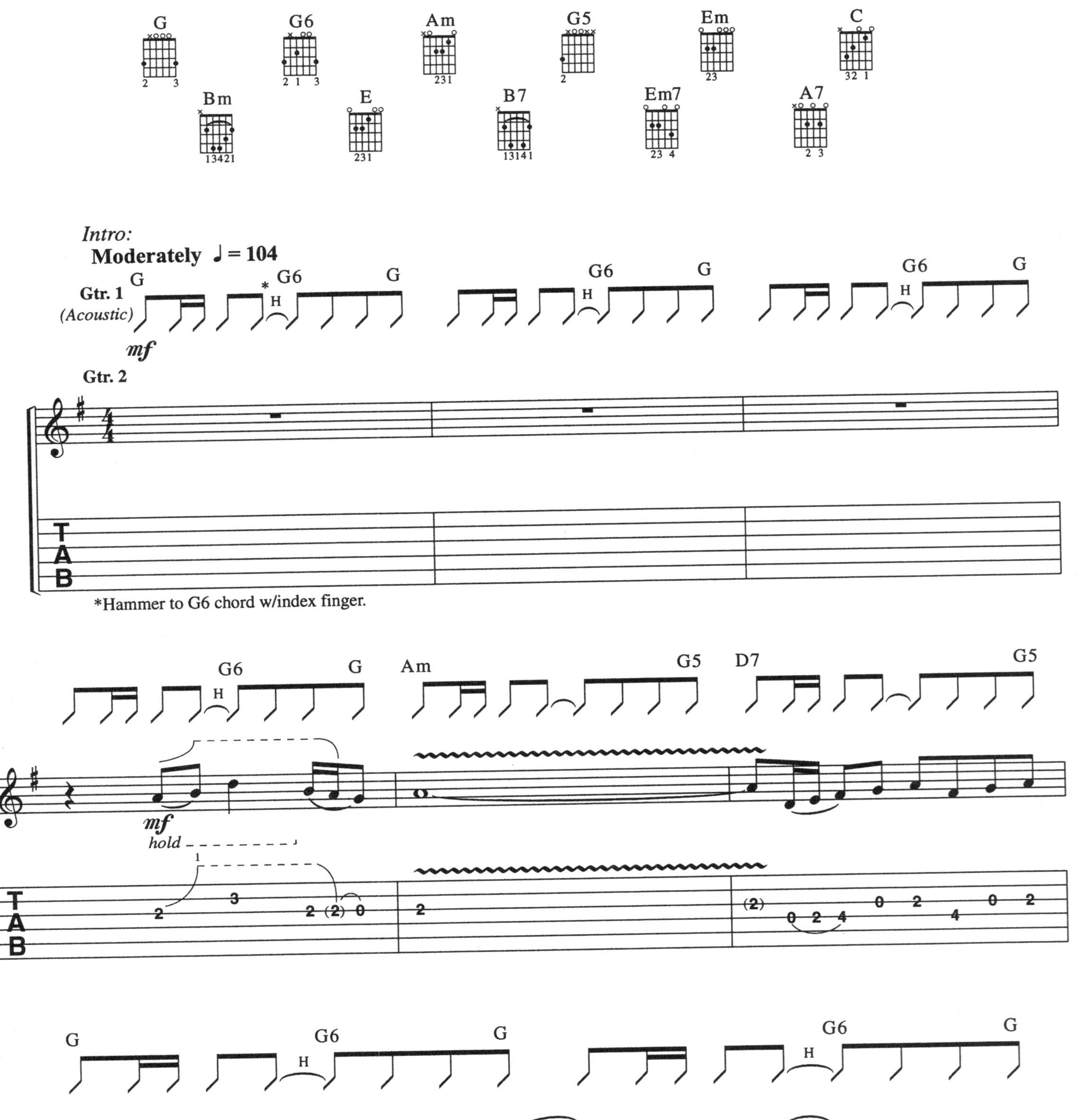

Verse 1:
Rhy. Fig. 1
D7
It's an - oth - er Te - qui - la Sun - rise, stir - ring slow -
hold
Am
G5
D7
G5
- ly 'cross the sky, they said good - bye.
trem. bar
G
G6
G
end Rhy. Fig. 1
G6
G
w/Rhy. Fig. 1 (Gtr. 1, 1st 6 bars only)
He was just a
harm.
(8va)
trem. bar
harm.

D7
hir - ed hand,
work - ing on a dream he'd planned to try;
Am
G5
D7
G5
G
the days go by.
trem. bar
Chorus:
Em
C
Em
Ev - 'ry night when the sun goes down,
Ooo.
trem. bar

C
Em
Ooo.
Just an - oth - er
lone - ly
boy
in town.
Ooo.
And
Am
D7
she's
out
run - nin' 'round.
harm.
hold
P.M.
harm.
Verse 2:
w/Rhy. Fig. 1 (Gtr. 1)
G
D7
She was - n't just an - oth - er wom - an,
and I could - n't
trem. bar
trem. bar

Am
D7
keep from com - in' on.
It's been so long.
trem. bar
G
G6
G
G6
G
w/Rhy. Fig. 1 (Gtr. 1, 1st 7 bars only)
Oh, and it's a
trem. bar
D7
hol - low feel - ing
when it comes down to deal - ing
Am
G5
D7
G5
G
G6
G
friends,
it nev - er ends.
trem. bar

Guitar Solo:
w/Rhy. Fig. 1 (Gtr. 1, 1st 6 bars only)
D7
hold
hold
Am
G5
D7
G5
G
Gtr. 1
Gtr. 2
Bridge:
Am
D7
Ooo. Take an - oth - er shot of cour - age,
hold

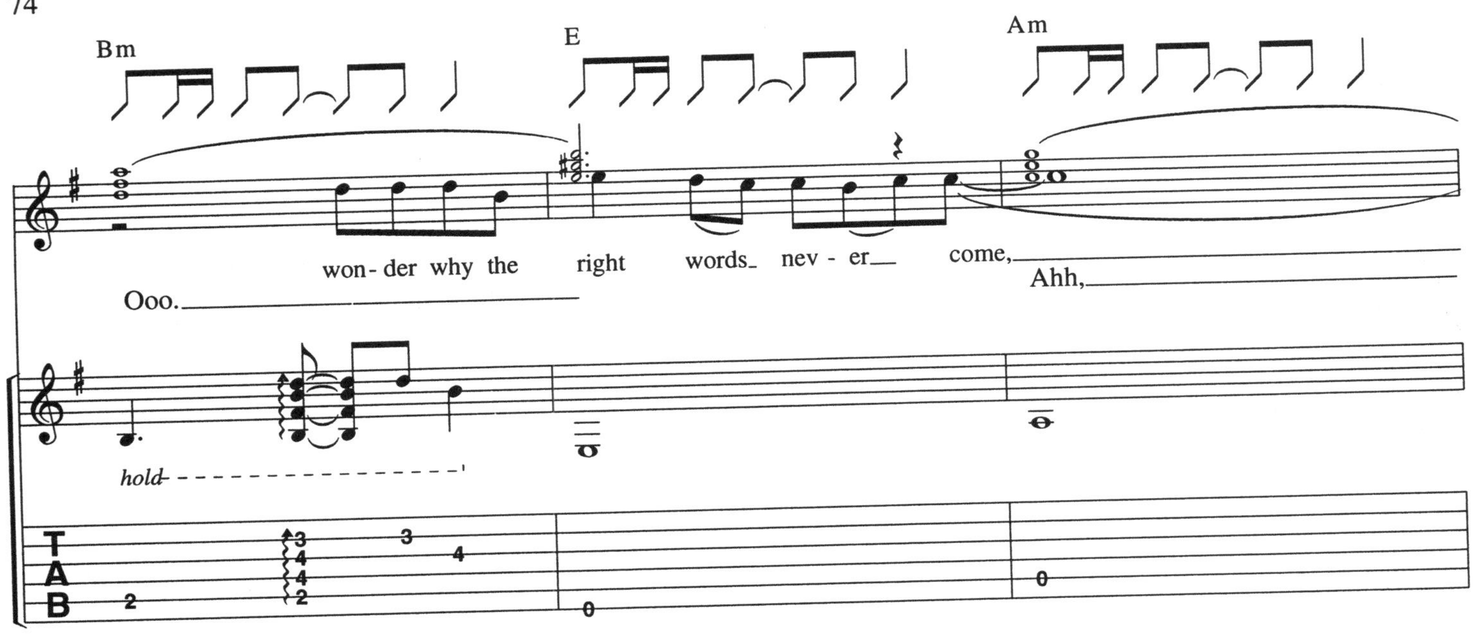
Bm
E
Am
wonder why the right words never come,
Ooo.
Ahh,
hold
T
A
B

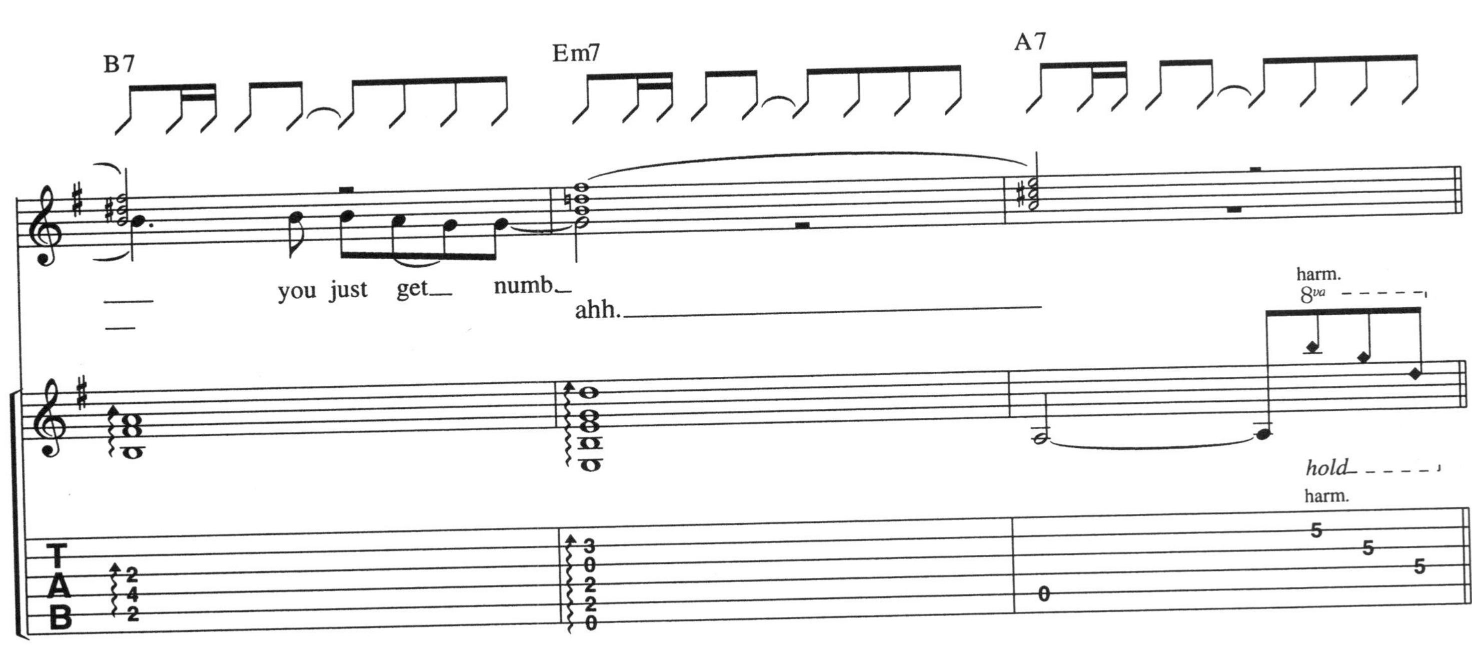
B7
Em7
A7
you just get numb
ahh.
harm.
8va
hold
harm.
T
A
B

Verse 3:
w/Rhy. Fig. 1 (Gtr. 1, 1st 6 bars only)
G
D7
It's another Tequila Sunrise this old world
hold
trem. bar
T
A
B

Am
G5
D7
G5
still
looks
the
same,
an - oth - er
friend.
trem. bar

G
Gtr. 1
Ooo.
Gtr. 2
hold
hold

hold
trem. bar

# hotel california

Words and Music by
DON HENLEY, GLENN FREY, DON FELDER

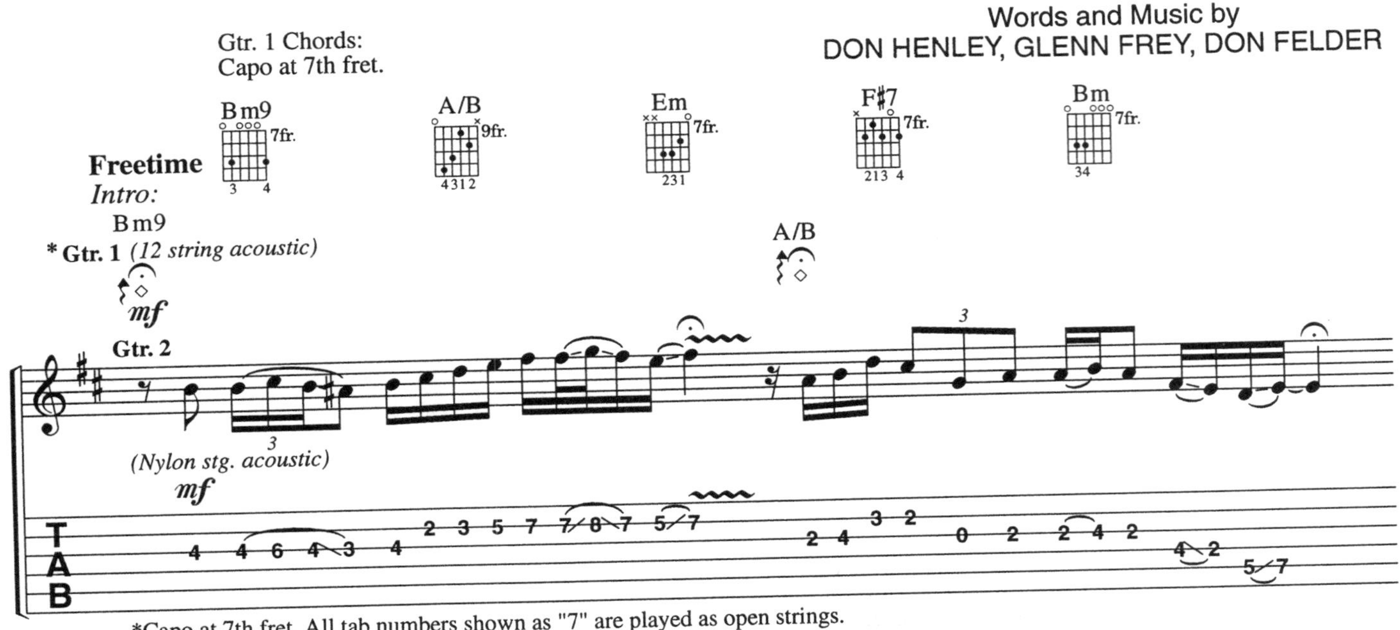


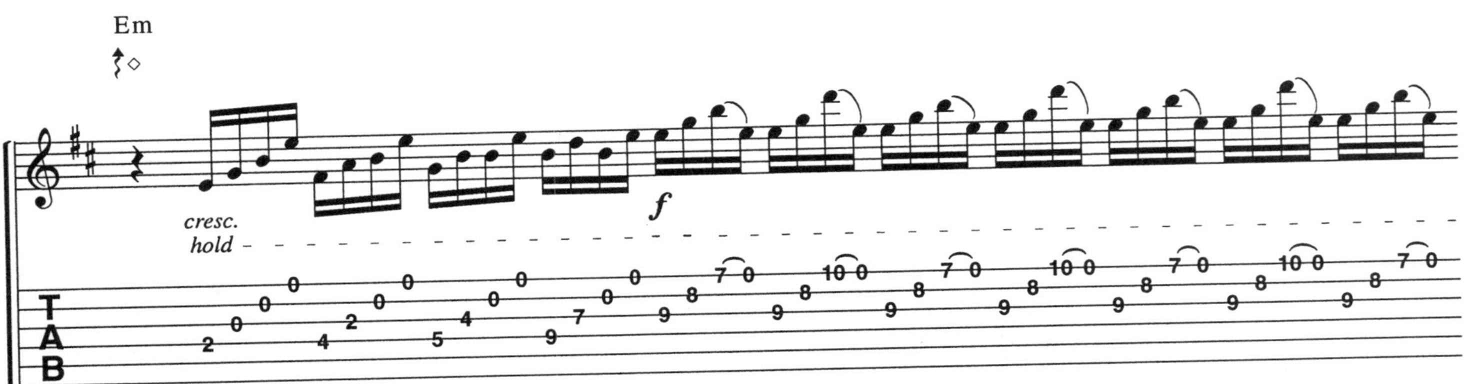


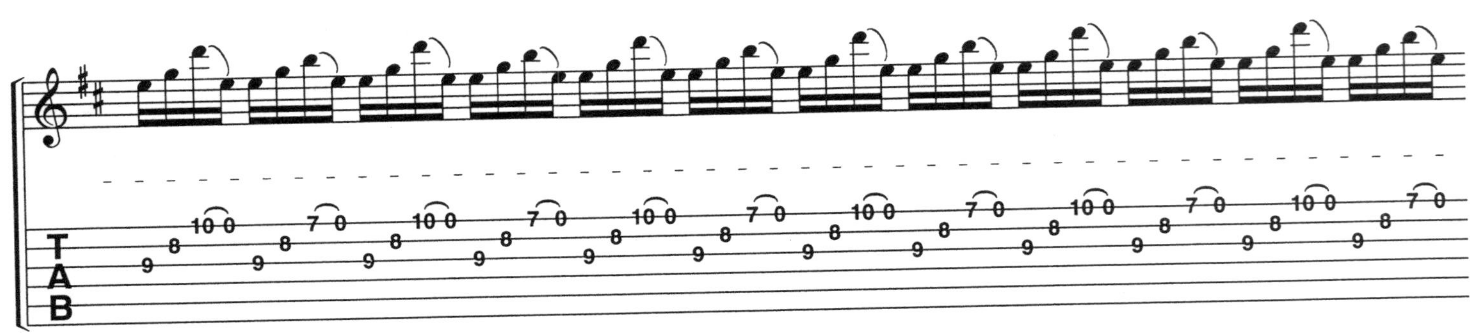

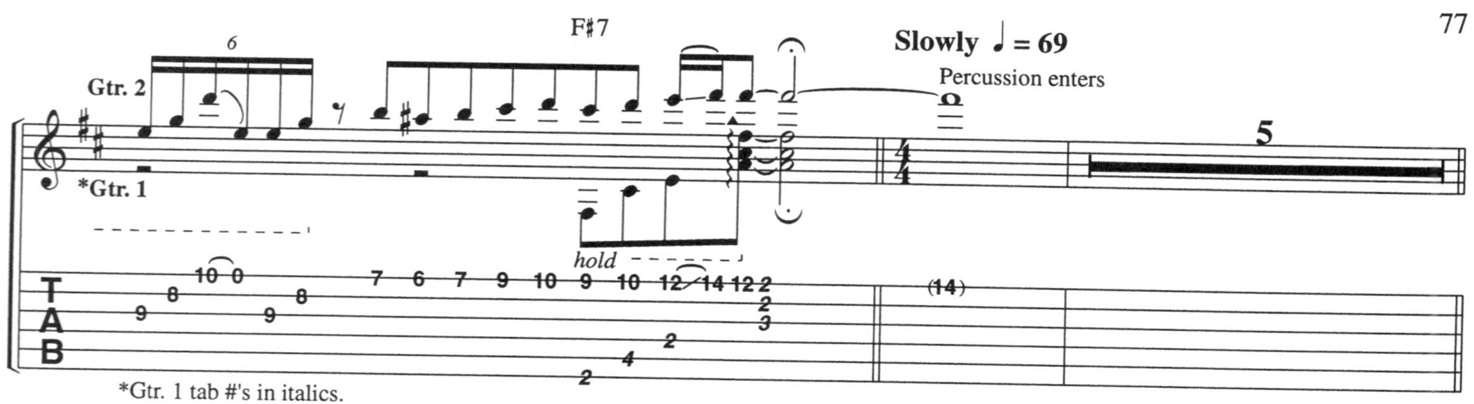
F♯7
Slowly ♩ = 69
Percussion enters
Gtr. 2
*Gtr. 1
hold
*Gtr. 1 tab #'s in italics.

Bm9
Gtr. 1
A/B

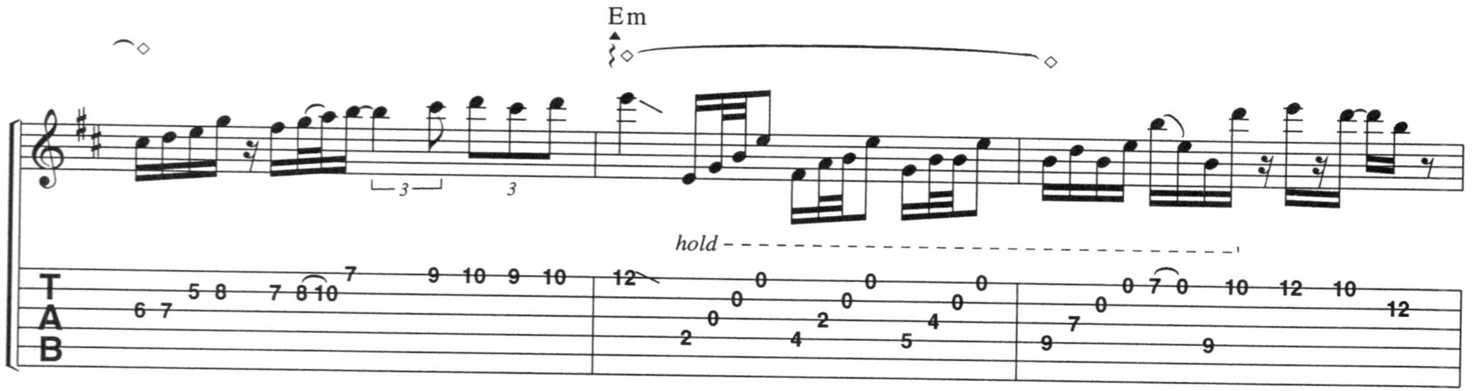
Em
hold

F♯7

Bm
F♯7/A♯
Asus2
Rhy. Fig. 1
Gtr. 1
f
hold throughout
Rhy. Fig. 1A
Gtr. 3 (6 string acoustic)
f
hold throughout
E9/G♯
G
D/F♯
Em7
F♯7
end Rhy. Fig. 1
end Rhy. Fig 1A

w/Rhy Fig. 1 (Gtr.1, simile)
Bm
Gtr. 4 (Nylon stg. acoustic)
F♯7
Asus2
f
Gtr. 3
E9
G
D
Em7
F♯

Verse 1:
w/Rhy. Fig. 1A (Gtr. 3, simile)
Bm
F♯7
On a dark des-ert high-way,
cool wind in my hair,
Gtr. 1
Asus2
E
warm smell of co-li-tas
ris-ing up thru' the air.
G
D
Up a-head in the dis-tance,
I saw a shim-mer-ing light,
Em7
F♯7
my head grew heav-y and my sight grew dim,
I had to stop for the night.

*Verse 2:
**w/Rhy. Figs. 1** *(Gtr.1)* & **1A** *(Gtr. 3) Both simile*

Bm
There she stood in the door-way, I heard a mis-sion bell;
Gtr. 2
*Gtr. 4 tacet

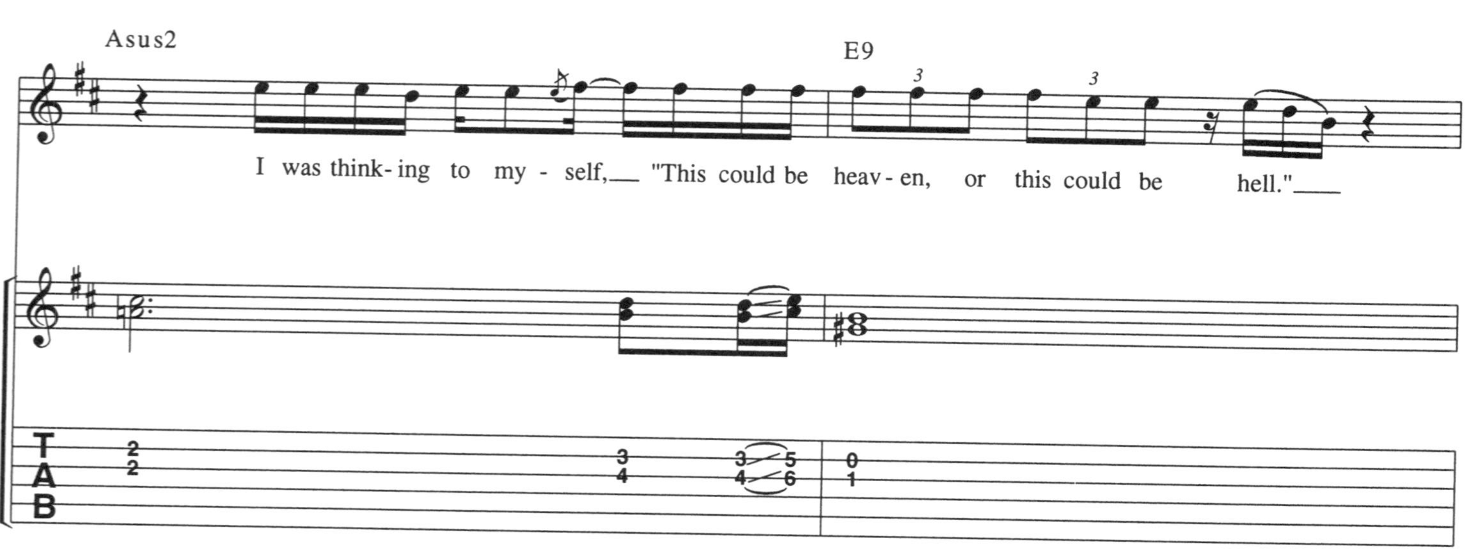

Asus2
E9
I was think-ing to my-self, "This could be heav-en, or this could be hell."

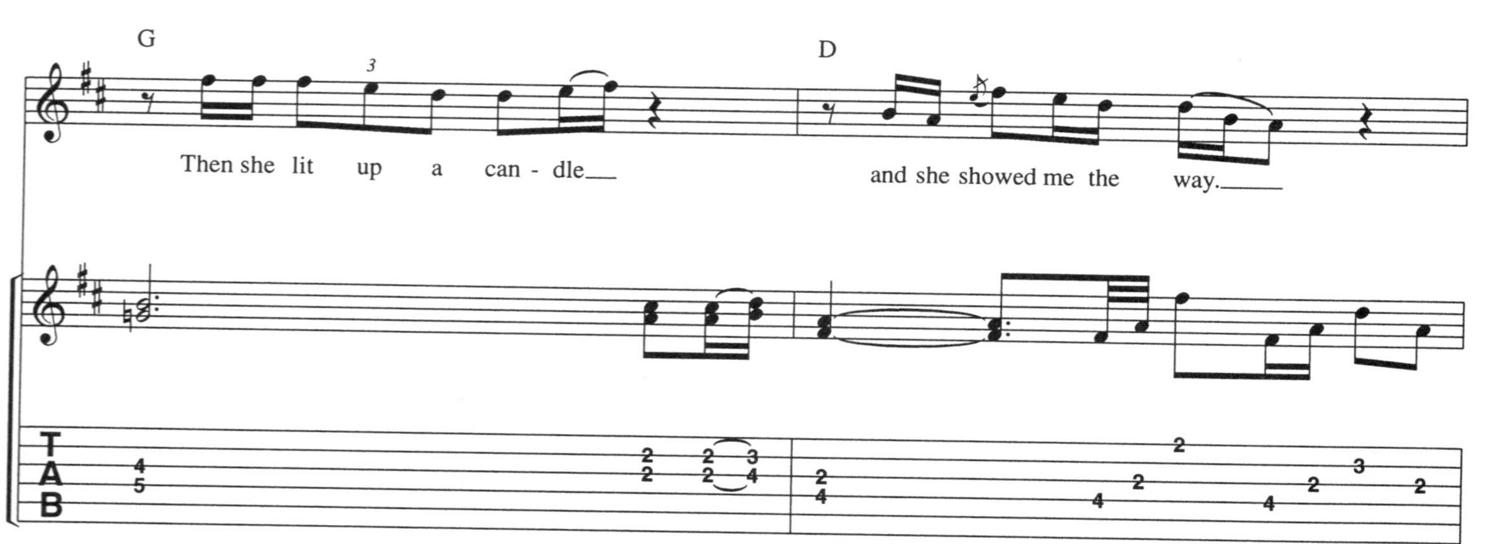

G
D
Then she lit up a can-dle and she showed me the way.

Em7 F#7

There were voic - es down the cor - ri - dor,___ *I* thought I heard them say;___

Gr. 1

Gtr. 4

*Chorus:*

G D

"Wel - come___ to the Ho - tel Cal - i - for - nia, such a

Rhy. Fig. 2

Gtr. 4

Gtr. 2

Gtr. 4

F♯7 Bm

love - ly place, such a love - ly place, such a love - ly face.

Gtr. 2

Gtr. 4

G D

Plen- ty of room at the Ho - tel Cal - i - for - nia, an - y

Gtr. 4

Em F♯7

time of year, an - y time of year, you can find it here.

end Rhy. Fig. 2

T A B 7 9 9 9 8 9 | 9 8 9 7 9 9

T A B | 2

*Verse 3:
w/Rhy. Figs. 1 *(Gtr. 1)* & 1A *(Gtr. 3) Both simile*

Bm F♯7

Her mind is Tif - fa - ny twist - ed, she got the Mer - ce - des bends, *uh.*

*Gtrs. 2 & 4 tacet.

Asus2 E9

She got a lot of pret- ty, pret- ty boys that she calls friends.

G D

How they dance in the court - yard, sweet sum - mer sweat.

Em7 F♯7

Some dance to re - mem - ber; some dance to for - get.

Verse 4:
w/Rhy. Figs. 1 (Gtr. 1) & 1A (Gtr. 3) Both simile
Bm
F#7
So I called up the Cap-tain, "Please bring me my wine." He said,
Gtr. 2
Asus2
E9
"We hav-en't had that spir-it here since nine-teen six-ty nine."
G
D
And still those voic-es are call-ing from far a-way.
Em7
F#7
Wake you up in the mid-dle of the night just to here them say;
Gtrs. 2 & 4
hold
hold

*Chorus:*

**w/Rhy. Fig. 2** *(Gtr.1, simile)*

G — D

"Wel-come to the Ho - tel Cal - i - for - nia, such a

Gtr. 2

F♯7 — Bm

love - ly place, such a love - ly place, such a love - ly face. They're

Gtr. 4 — Gtr. 2

*hold*

G — D

liv-in' it up at the Ho - tel Cal - i - for - nia. What a

Gtr. 2

Em — F♯7

nice sur - prise, what a nice sur - prise. Bring your al - i - bis."

*hold*

*Verse 5:
w/Rhy. Figs. 1 (Gtr.1) & 1A (Gtr. 2) Both simile
Bm
F#7
Mir - rors on the ceil - ing, the pink cham - pagne on ice, and she said,
*Gtrs. 2 & 4 tacet.
Asus2
E9
"We are all just pris - on - ers here, of our own de - vice."
G
D
And in the mas - ter's cham - bers they gath - ered for the feast.
Em7
F#7
They stab it with their steel - y knives, but they just can't kill the beast.
Verse 6:
w/Rhy. Figs. 1 (Gtr.1) & 1A (Gtr. 2) Both simile
Bm
F#7
Last thing I re - mem - ber, I was run - ning for the door.
Gtr. 2
Asus2
E9
I had to find the pas - sage back to the place I was be - fore.

G
D
"Re - lax," said the night - man, "we are pro - grammed to re - cieve.
Em7
F#7
You can check out an - y time you like, but you can nev - er leave."
Gtr. 4
Guitar Solo I:
w/Rhy. Figs. 1 (Gtr. 1) & 1A (Gtr. 3) Both 3 times, simile
Bm
F#7
Asus2
E9
G
D
harm.

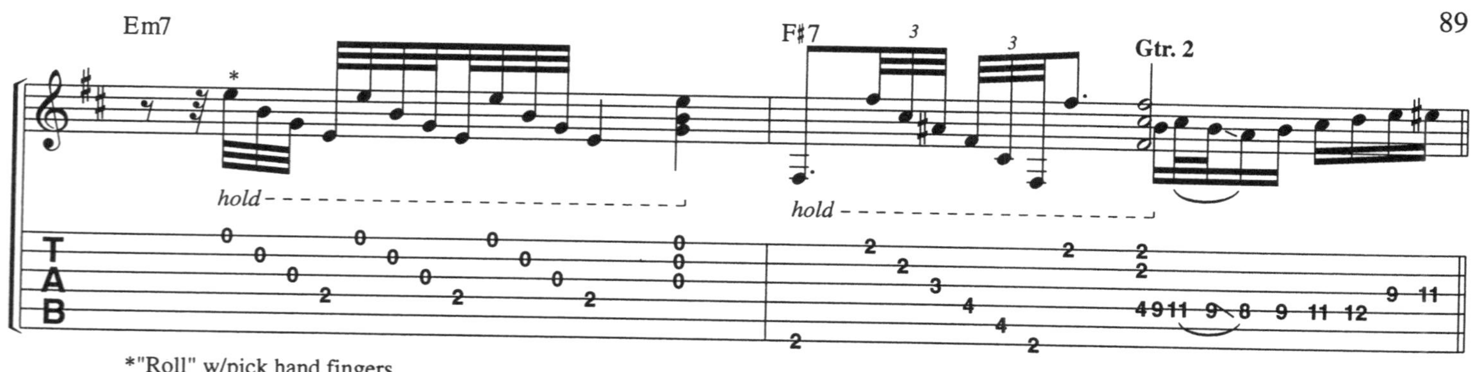


*"Roll" w/pick hand fingers

*Guitar Solo II:*

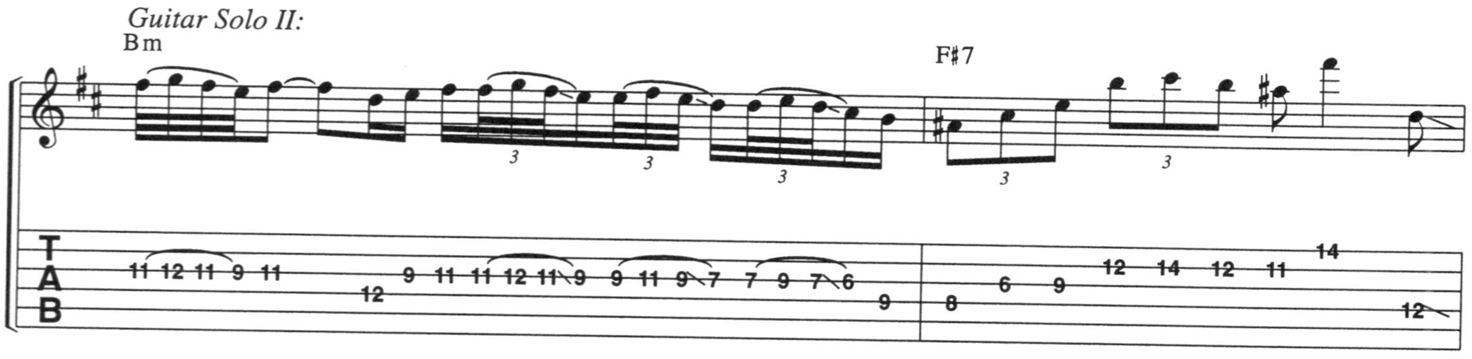


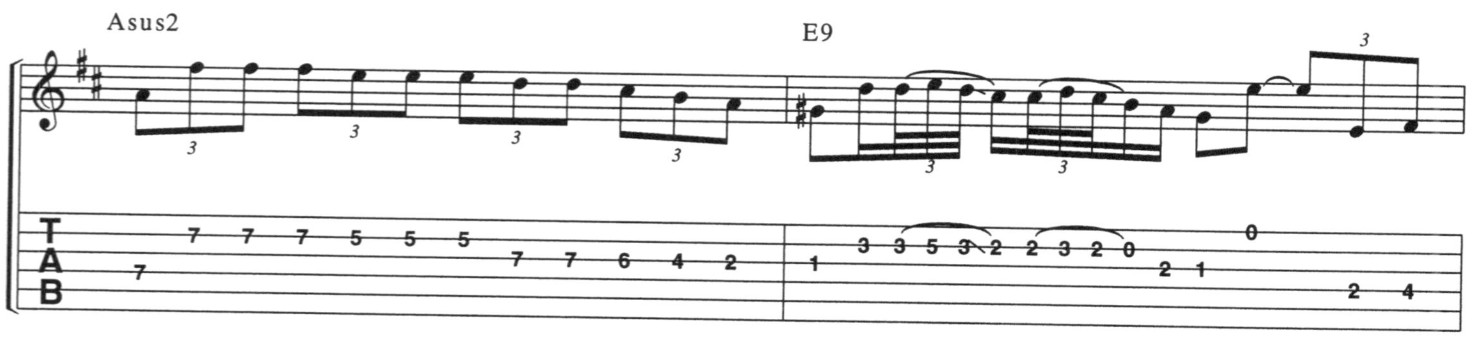

Em7
F#7
Gtr. 4
Outro:
Bm
F#7
Asus2
E9

Em7 F♯7 Bm

# wasted time

Words and Music by
DON HENLEY and GLENN FREY

*Intro:*
**Slowly ♩ = 60 Rock ballad**

C
Fm6
C/G
G9(3)
G
G7sus
Gtr. 1*
hold throughout
mf
Thumb

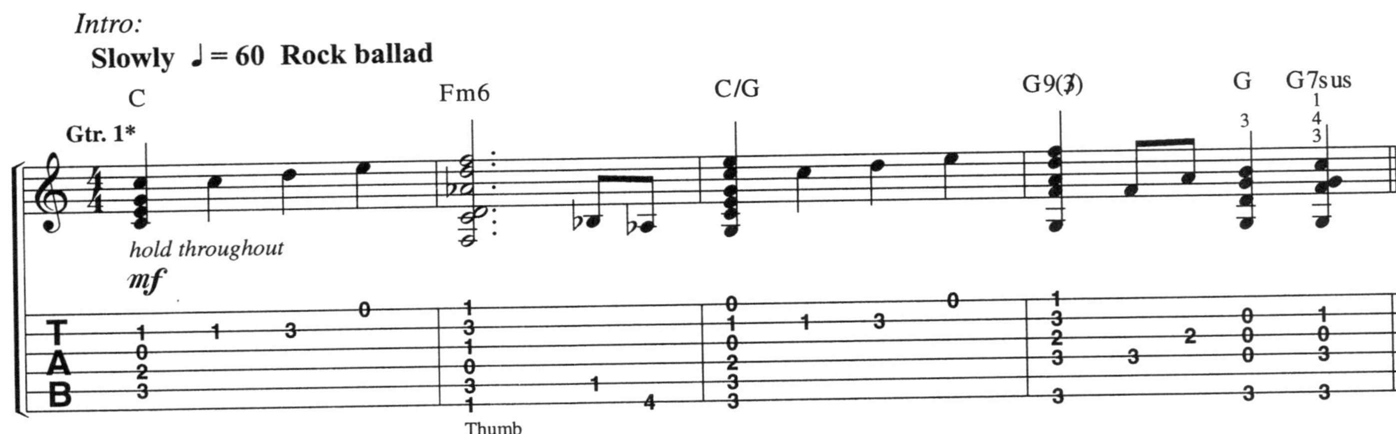

*Optional: pianos arranged for gtr. Combine fingerstyle w/strumming.

*Verse 1:*

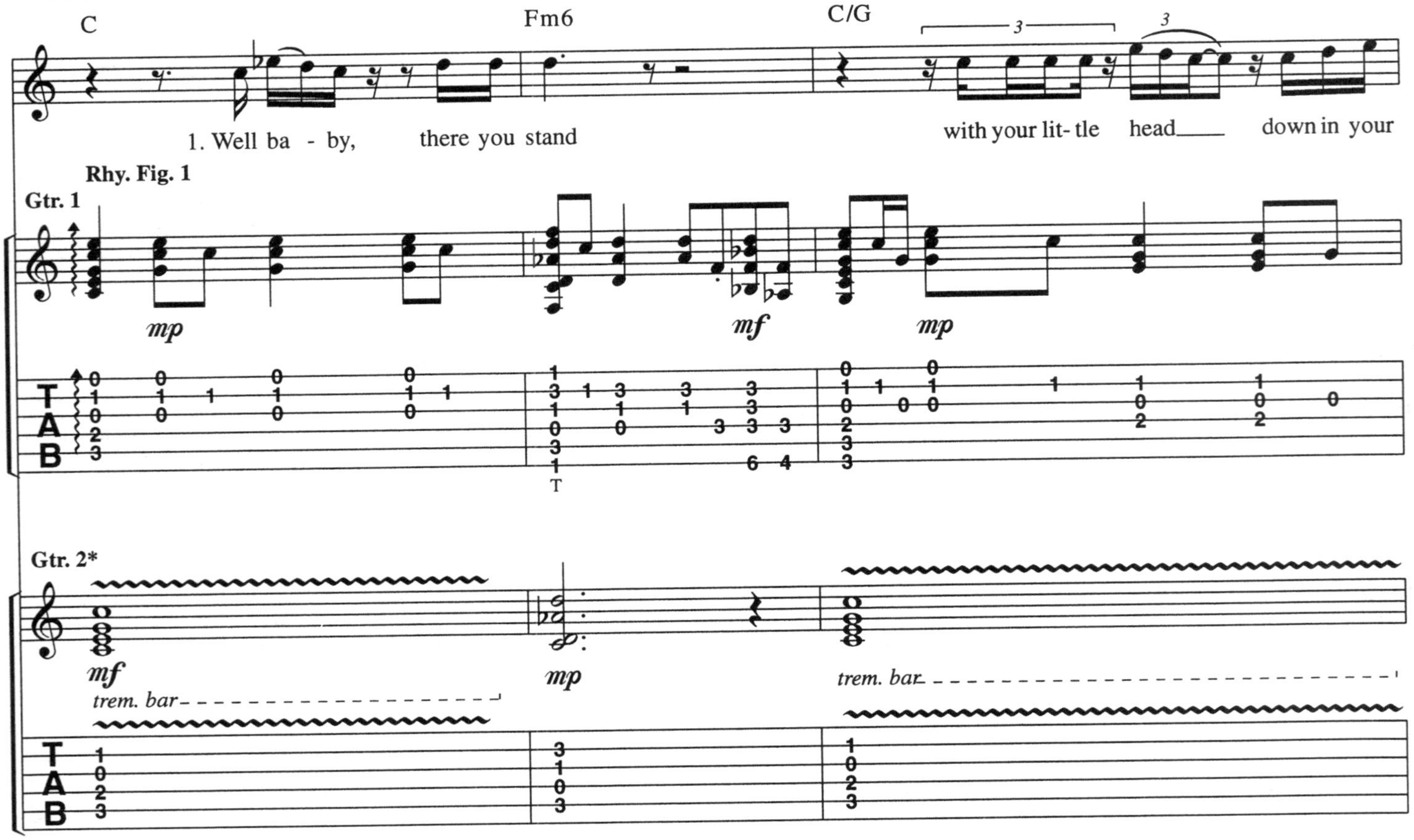

C
Fm6
C/G
1. Well ba - by, there you stand with your lit- tle head down in your
Rhy. Fig. 1
Gtr. 1
mp
mf
mp
T
Gtr. 2*
mf
mp
trem. bar
trem. bar

*Electric Gtr. (clean tone w/chorus effect).

F/G G7 F C/E Dm9 C/E
hands. Oh my God, you can't be-lieve it's hap-pen-ing a-gain. Your
F C/E Dm9 F/G G7
ba - by's gone and you're all a - lone and it looks like the end.
end Rhy. Fig. 1
T
A
B

Verse 2:
w/Rhy. Fig. 1 cont. simile:
C
Fm6
C/G
2. Your back out on the street, and you're try - in' to re-
Gr. 2
mf
mem- ber, oh.
F
G7
Strings enter
F
C/E
Dm7
C/E
How do you start it o- ver? You don't know if you can. You
F
C/E
Dm9
ritard.
F/G
G7
don't care much for a stran - ger's touch but you can't hold your man.
Interlude:
Freely*
Am
E7/G♯
G
D/F♯
F
(You) nev- er thought you'd be a- lone this far down the line. But I know what's been on your
Gtr. 1 (Piano)
*Vocal and piano alone.

*With distortion and echo next four measures.

**Echo

Am
Bm7
E7
Am
Am/G
fell, fell._
You did-n't love___ the boy__ too much.
No, no,_ you just
mf
Fmaj7
C/E
ritard.
Fm6/D
G11
G7
loved___ the boy too___ well,
well,___ well, well.

*Vocal and piano alone.

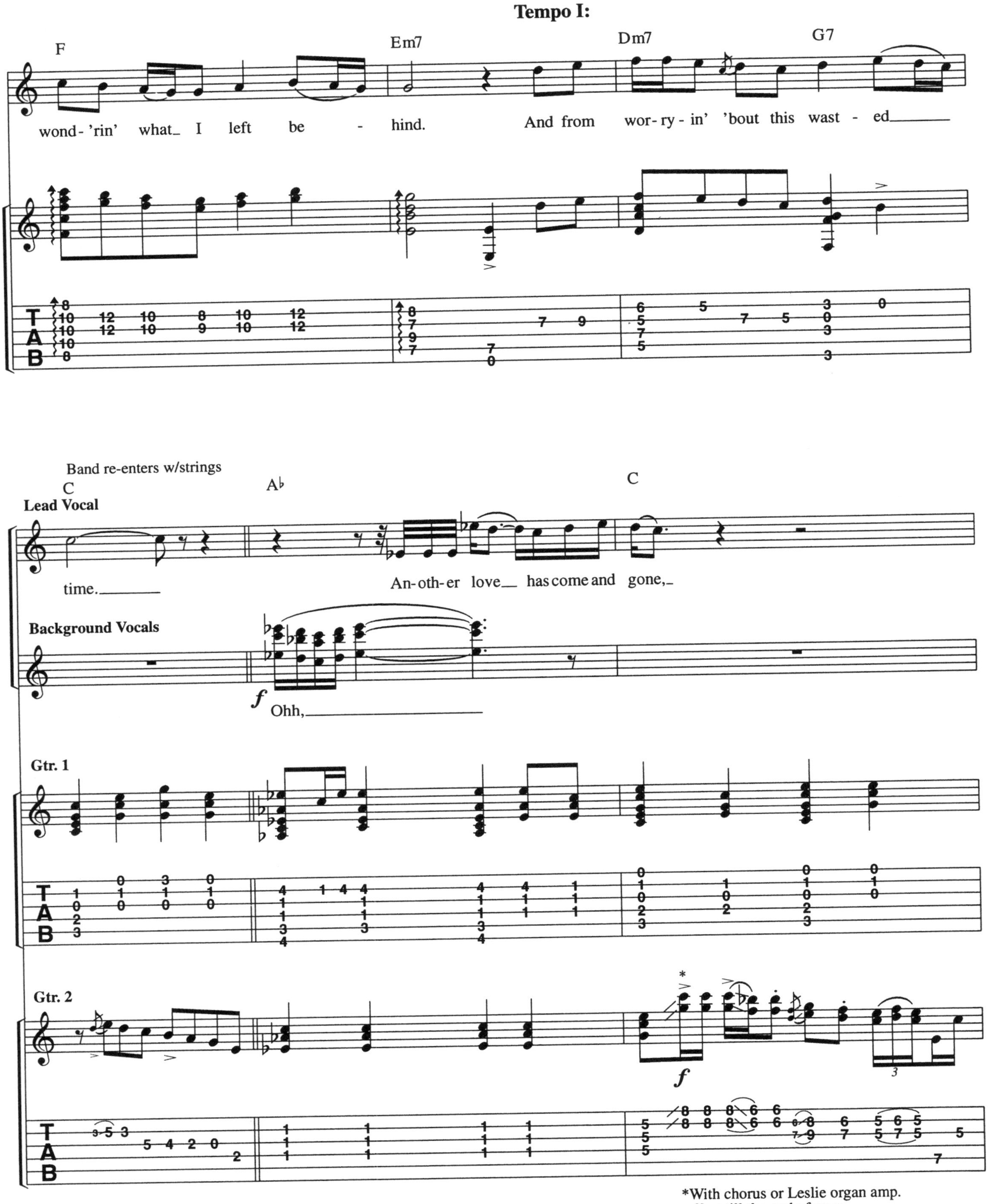

Band re-enters w/strings

C Ab C

**Lead Vocal**

time.___ An-oth-er love__ has come and gone,_

**Background Vocals**

*f* Ohh,___

**Gtr. 1**

**Gtr. 2**

*f*

*With chorus or Leslie organ amp. effect till the end of song.

A♭
C
Dm7
Em
and the years keep rush- ing on.
I re -
Ohh,
mf
F
C/E
Dm7
C/E
mem- ber what you told me
be- fore you went out on your own.
"Some- times to
Ah,

ritard.
F
C/E
Dm9
G7
G♯dim
keep it to-geth-er we got to leave it a-lone." So
Ah,
Interlude:
Freely*
Am
E7/G♯
G
D/F♯
you can get on with your search ba-by, and I can get on with mine. And
Gtr. 1
*Vocal and piano alone.
add strings**
Tempo I:
F
Em7
Dm7
G11
G7
may-be some-day we will find, that it was-n't real-ly wast-ed
**Upbeat of "one" (crescendo).

Band re-enters

C C/E Fmaj7 C/G A♭ C C/E Fmaj7 C/G

time. Ooh, ooh, ooh, oh,

Gtr. 1

Gtr. 2

A♭ B♭ C C/E Fmaj7 C/G A♭ Fm9 Fm$^{6}_{9}$ C

*ritard.*

ooh, ooh, ooh, ooh, ooh, ooh, ooh.

# i can't tell you why

Words and Music by
DON HENLEY, GLENN FREY and TIMOTHY B. SCHMIT

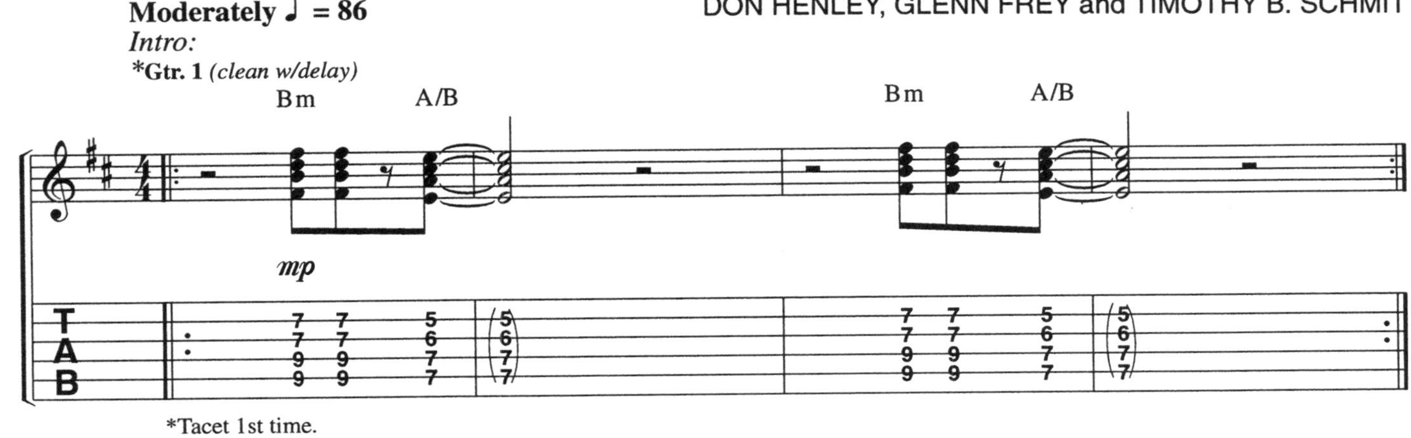

I Can't Tell You Why - 6 - 1
PG9513

* Secondary vocal tacet 1st time.

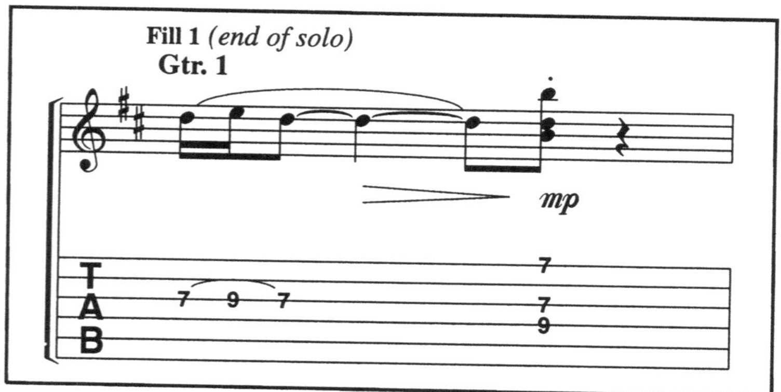

1. Chorus:
Bm
A(9)/B
N.C.
(Gmaj7)
Gmaj7 F♯m7
can't tell you why.
2. Chorus:
Bm
A(9)/B
Gmaj7
can't tell you why,
no, ba - by, I can't tell you why.
F♯sus
F♯7
Gmaj7
To Coda
F♯m11
N.C.
I can't tell you why.
(Bm)
A/B
N.C.
(Bm)
A/B
*mf
*Slightly overdriven.

Guitar Solo:
*N.C.(Dmaj7)
(Gmaj7)
Ooh.
* Accompaniment provided by keyboard and strings.
(Dmaj7)
Ooh.
(Gmaj7)
(F♯7sus)
(F♯7)
D.S. 𝄋 al Coda
(take 2nd ending)
Ooh.
hold
Coda
F♯m11
Gmaj7
F♯m11
I can't tell you why.
No.
Oh, oh.

Outro Solo:
N.C. (Gmaj7)
F♯m7
Gmaj7
F♯m7
Gmaj7
F♯m7
Gmaj7
F♯m7
hold
Gmaj7
F♯m7
Gmaj7
hold
F♯m7
Gmaj7
F♯m7
Gmaj7
F♯m7
Gmaj7

*Verse 2:*
When we get crazy it just ain't right, girl,
I get lonely too.
You don't have to worry, just hold on tight
'Cause I love you.

*Pre-Chorus 2:*
Nothing's wrong as far as I can see.
We make it harder than it has to be.

# new york minute

Words and Music by
DON HENLEY, DANNY KORTCHMAR and JAI WINDING

*Keyboard arranged for fingerstyle guitar.

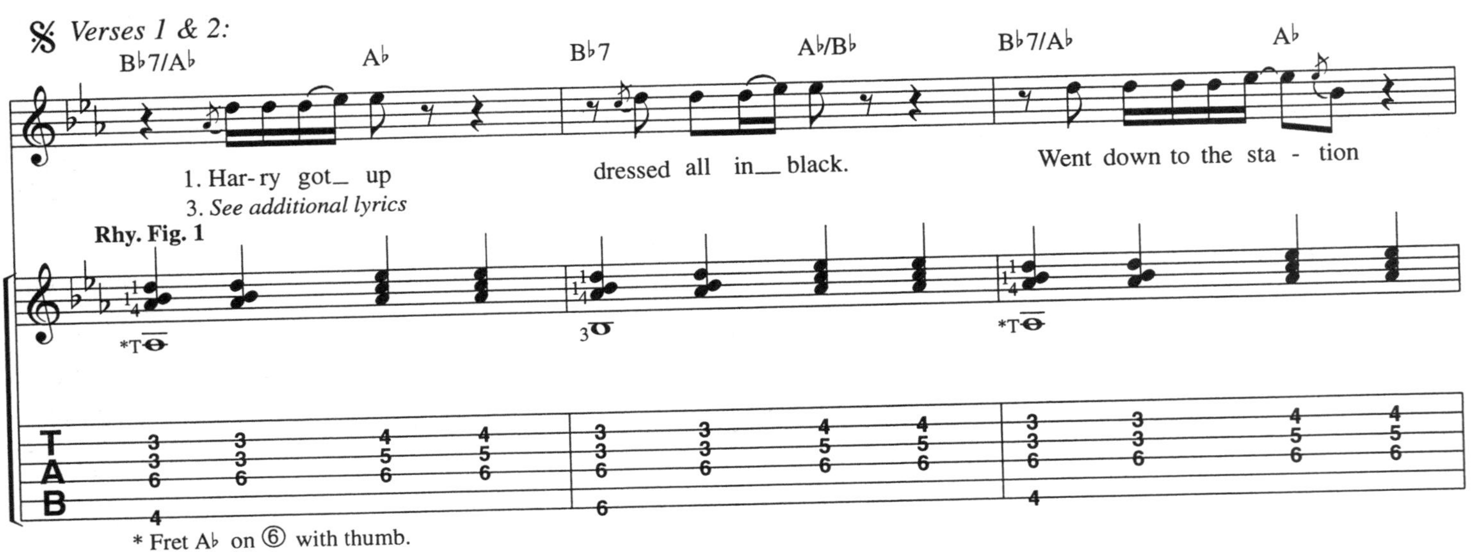


* Fret A♭ on ⑥ with thumb.

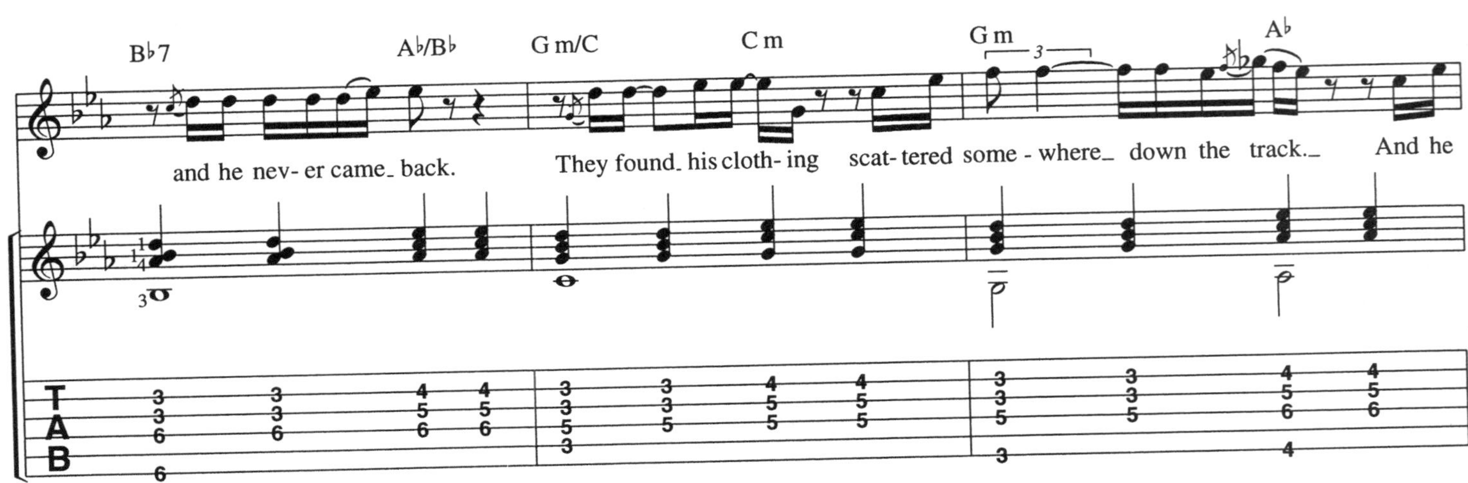

F7/A
G7/B
B♭/C
Cm7
won't be___ down on Wall Street___ in the morn - ing.___
end Rhy. Fig. 1
w/Rhy. Fig. 1 (Gtr. 1)
B♭7/A♭
A♭
B♭7
A♭/B♭
He had a home,___ love of a girl.___ But men get lost some-times___
as years un - furl.
Gm/C
Cm
One___ day he crossed___ some line___ and he was
Gm
too much___ in this world.___ But I guess it___ does-n't mat-ter___ an-y-more.___
Chorus: Rhy. Fig. 2
Gtr. 3
(w/distortion)
G5
A♭5
B♭5
C5
end Rhy. Fig. 2
In a
New___ York min-ute... Ooh.___ ev - 'ry-thing can change.___
Rhy. Fig. 2A
Gtr. 1
end Rhy. Fig. 2A
Rhy. Fig. 2B
*Gtr. 2
end Rhy. Fig. 2B
hold
*Clean electric with chorus, delay and compression.

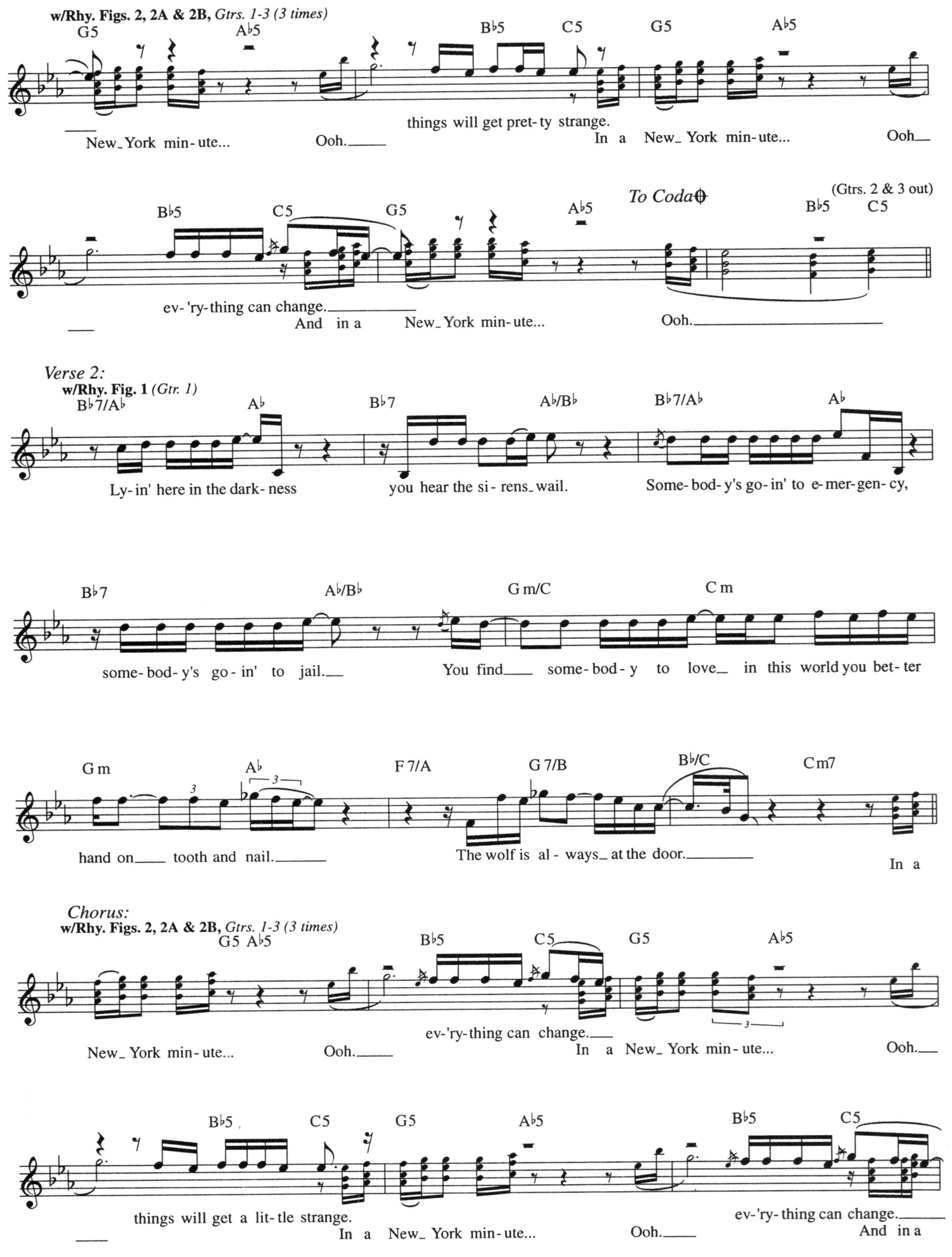
w/Rhy. Figs. 2, 2A & 2B, Gtrs. 1-3 (3 times)
G5 A♭5 B♭5 C5 G5 A♭5
New_York min-ute... Ooh.___ things will get pret-ty strange. In a New_York min-ute... Ooh___
To Coda
(Gtrs. 2 & 3 out)
B♭5 C5 G5 A♭5 B♭5 C5
ev-'ry-thing can change.___ And in a New_York min-ute... Ooh.___
Verse 2:
w/Rhy. Fig. 1 (Gtr. 1)
B♭7/A♭ A♭ B♭7 A♭/B♭ B♭7/A♭ A♭
Ly-in' here in the dark-ness you hear the si-rens_wail. Some-bod-y's go-in' to e-mer-gen-cy,
B♭7 A♭/B♭ G m/C C m
some-bod-y's go-in' to jail.___ You find___ some-bod-y to love_ in this world you bet-ter
G m A♭ F 7/A G 7/B B♭/C C m7
hand on___ tooth and nail.___ The wolf is al-ways_at the door.___ In a
Chorus:
w/Rhy. Figs. 2, 2A & 2B, Gtrs. 1-3 (3 times)
G5 A♭5 B♭5 C5 G5 A♭5
New_York min-ute... Ooh.___ ev-'ry-thing can change.___ In a New_York min-ute... Ooh.___
B♭5 C5 G5 A♭5 B♭5 C5
things will get a lit-tle strange. In a New_York min-ute... Ooh.___ ev-'ry-thing can change.___ And in a

G5
Gtr. 3
A♭5
New_ York min-ute...
Ooh,
ooh
Gtr. 1
Gtr. 2
hold
Interlude:
Fm7
Dm7(♭5)
G7sus
G
Csus
C m
ooh.
And in these_ days,
when dark-ness falls_ ear-ly
Gtr. 1
Fm7
Dm7(♭5)
G7sus
G
Csus
C m
F7/A
G 7/B
and peo-ple rush_ home_
to the ones they love,_
you_ bet-ter take a fool's_ ad-vice

C m
B♭m
A♭7
Dm7(♭5)
E♭m7(♭5)
Dm7(♭5)
G7(♯5)
and take care of your___ own.
'Cause one day they're here,___ next day they're gone.___

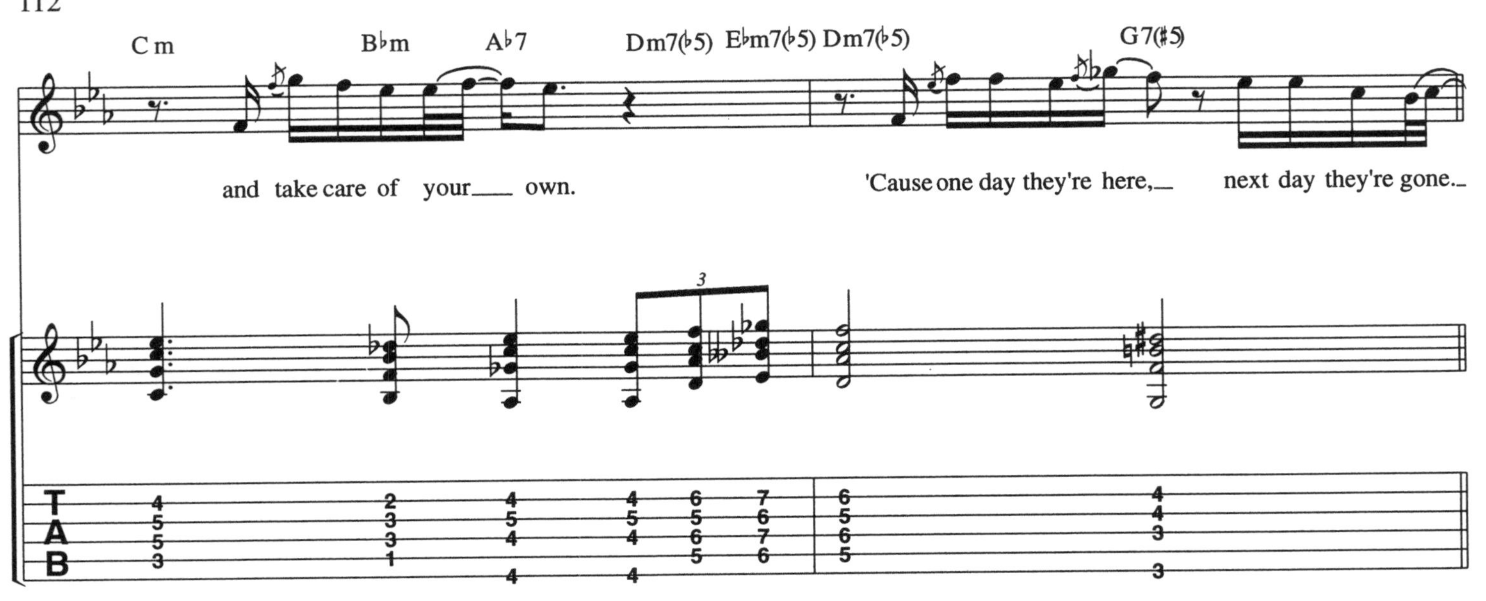

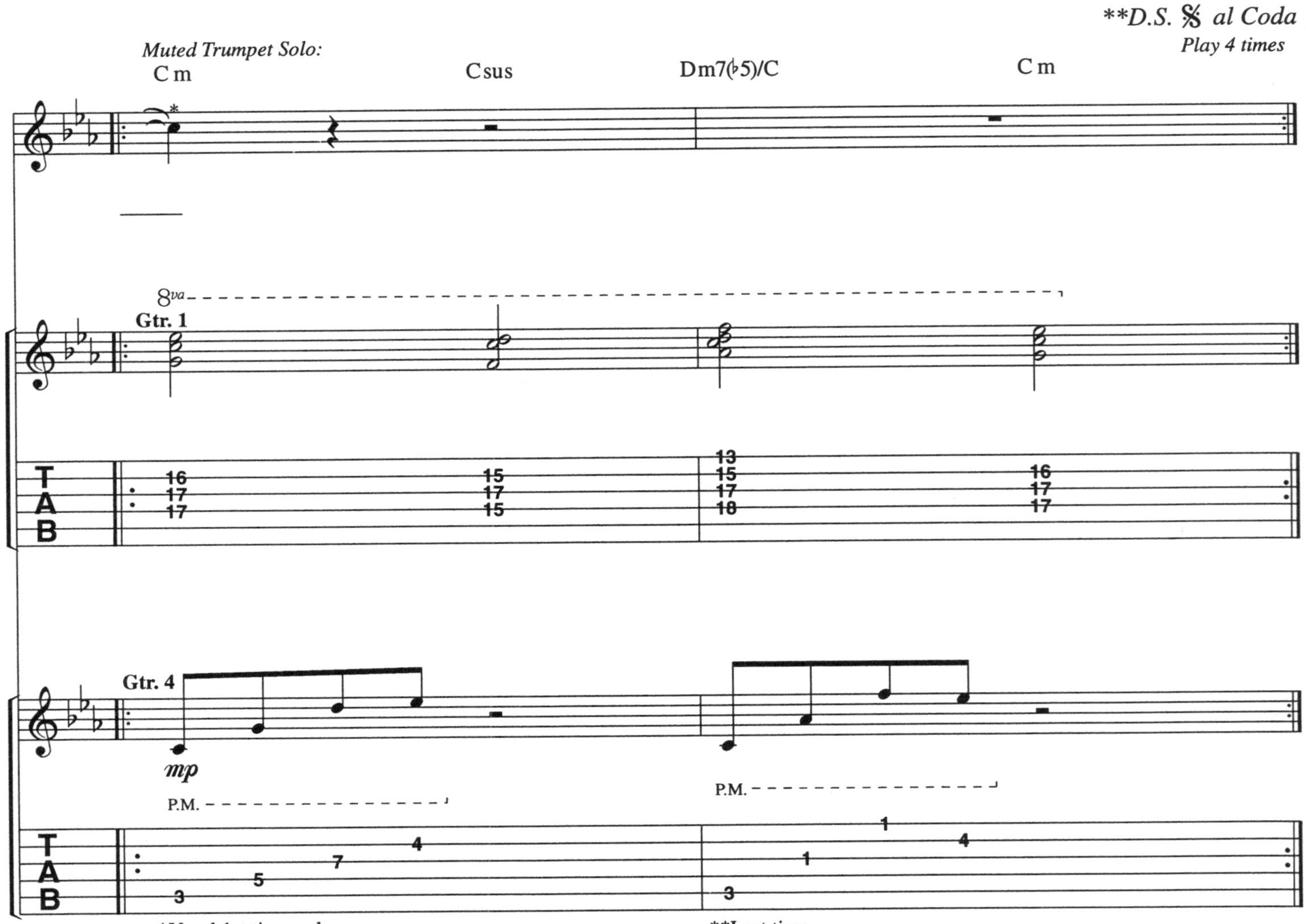

**D.S. 𝄋 al Coda
Play 4 times
Muted Trumpet Solo:
C m
Csus
Dm7(♭5)/C
C m
8va
Gtr. 1
Gtr. 4
mp
P.M.
P.M.

*Vocal 1st time only.

**Last time.

*Fading echo repeats.

*Verse 2:*
Pulled my coat around my shoulders and I took a walk down through the park.
The leaves were falling around me, the groaning city in the gathering dark.
And on some solitary rock a desperate lover left his mark.
He said, "Baby, I've changed. Please come back."
What the head makes cloudy the heart makes very clear.
I know the days were so much brighter in the time she was here.
But I know there's somebody somewhere make these dark clouds disappear.
But until that day I have to believe.
I believe...I believe.

# the last resort

Words and Music by
DON HENLEY and GLENN FREY

*Substitute the A major fingering as in measure one of this section in all future applications of this figure.

*Gtr. 2 Acoustic, Gtr. 3 Electric.

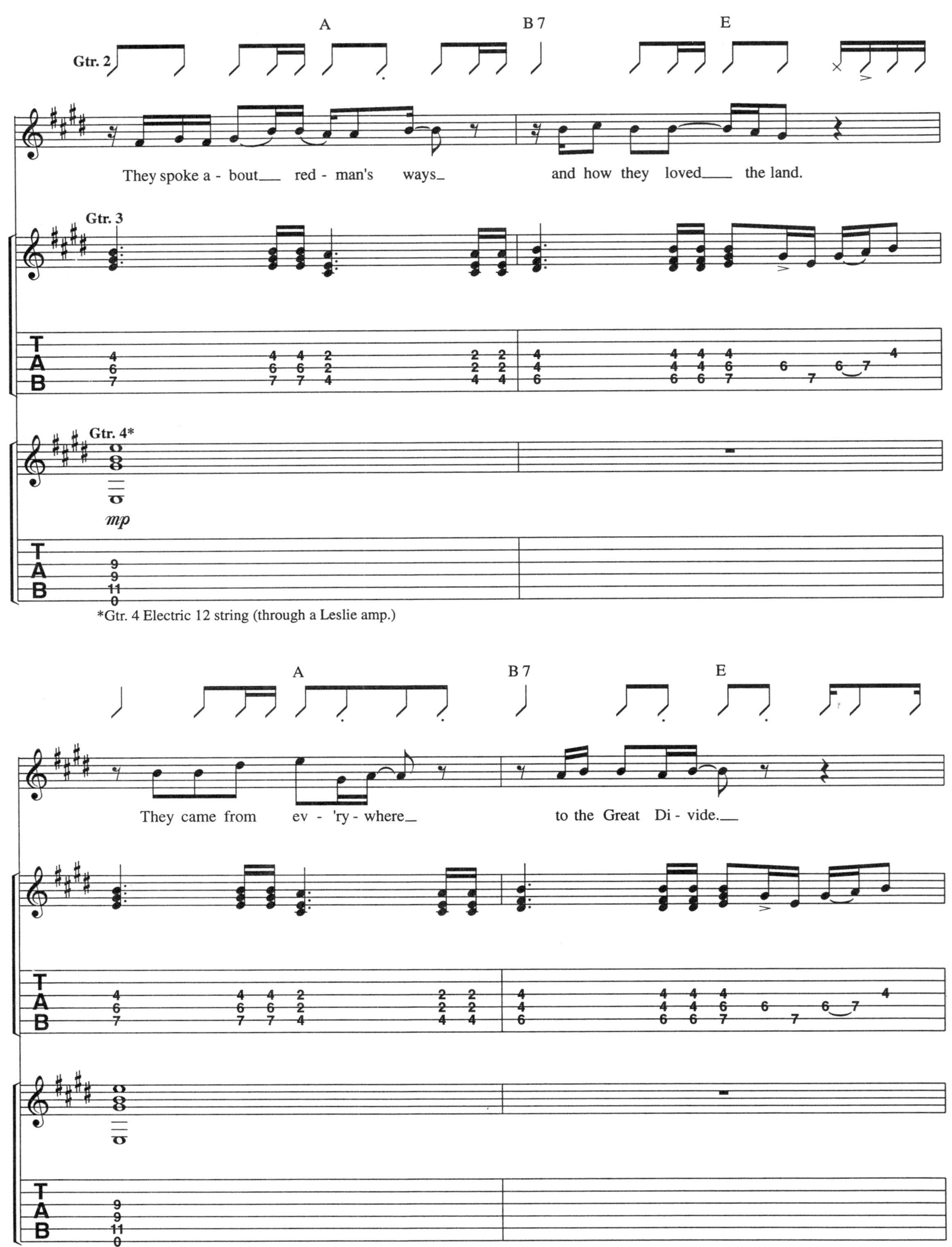
A
B 7
E
Gtr. 2
They spoke a - bout___ red - man's ways_
and how they loved___ the land.
Gtr. 3
Gtr. 4*
mp
*Gtr. 4 Electric 12 string (through a Leslie amp.)
They came from ev - 'ry - where_
to the Great Di - vide.___

A
B 7
E
Esus
Seek - ing a place to stand
or a place to hide.
Verse:
E
A
B 7
E
Down in the crowd - ed bars
out for a good time;
Rhy. Fig. 2

A
B 7
E
can't wait to tell you all
what it's like up there.
A
B 7
E
They call it par - a - dise,
I don't know why?

Rhy. Fig. 1 (Gtr. 1 ) out
A
B 7
E
Esus
Some- bod- y laid the moun- tains low__ while the town got__ high.
end Rhy. Fig. 2
Bridge 1:
Amaj7
A6
E
Esus
Amaj7
A

Gtr. 3 switches to pedal steel:
(B7
B11)*
E
Gtr. 2
Gtr. 1
mp
*Piano chords.
Verse:
Rhy. Figs. 1 and 2 cont. simile:
A
B
And then the chil - ly winds blew down across the des - ert,
Gtr. 5* (right channel)
slow slide
hold throughout
hold
*Pedal steel guitar arranged for electric guitar.
**Sideways vibrato.
through the can - yons of the coast to the Mal - i - bu.
choke
mf

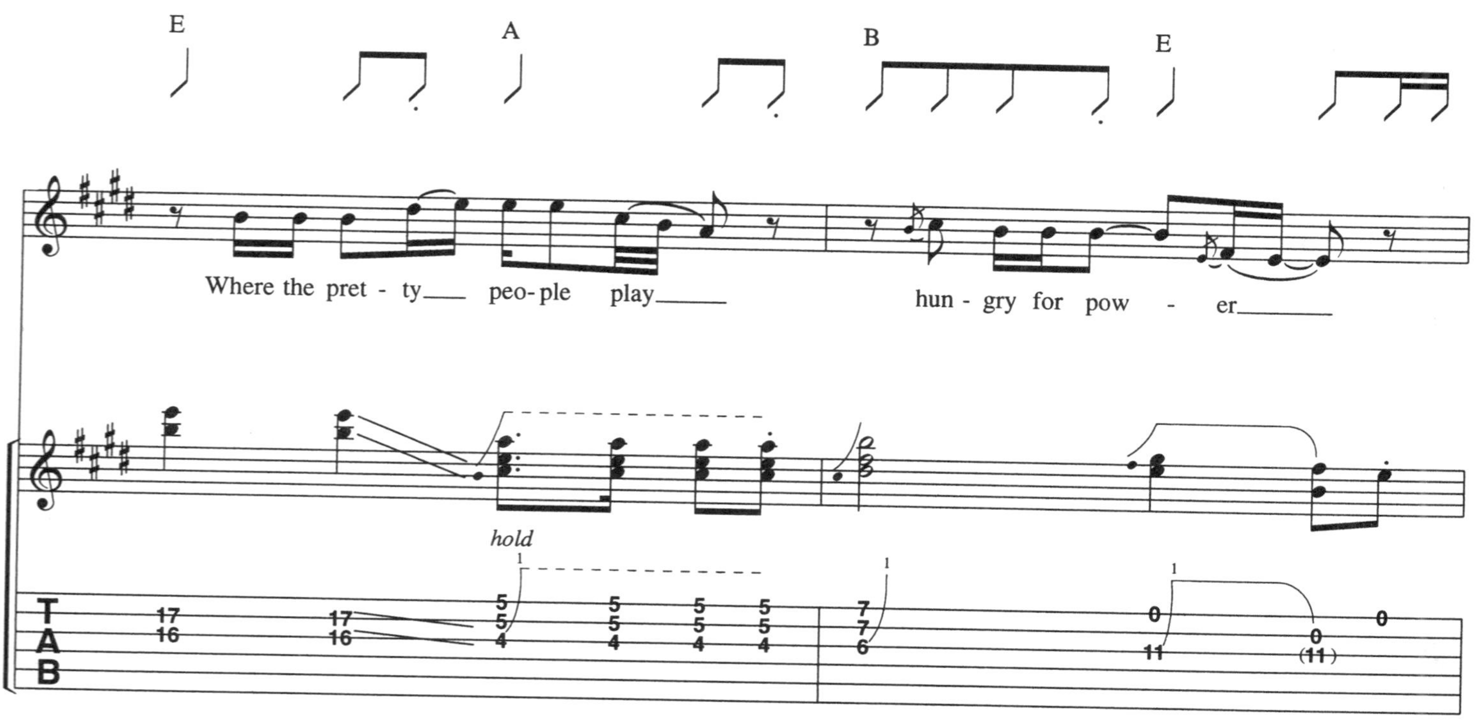
E
A
B
E
Where the pret - ty___ peo-ple play_____ hun - gry for pow - er_______
hold

A
B
E
Esus
to light_ their ne - on way_ give 'em things to do._______
hold
mf

Verse:
Rhy. Fig. 1 cont. simile
E
A
B
E
Some rich men came and raped the land, nobody caught 'em.
Gtr. 4
mf
Gtr. 5
hold
A
B
E
'Put up a bunch of ugly boxes, Jesus people bought 'em.

E
A
B
E
They called it par - a - dise;
the place to be.
A
B
E
end Rhy. Fig. 1
Esus
They watched the haz - y sun
sink-ing in the sea.

Bridge 2:
Amaj7
A6
harm.
E
Esus
Amaj7
A6
mf
f
mf
TAB

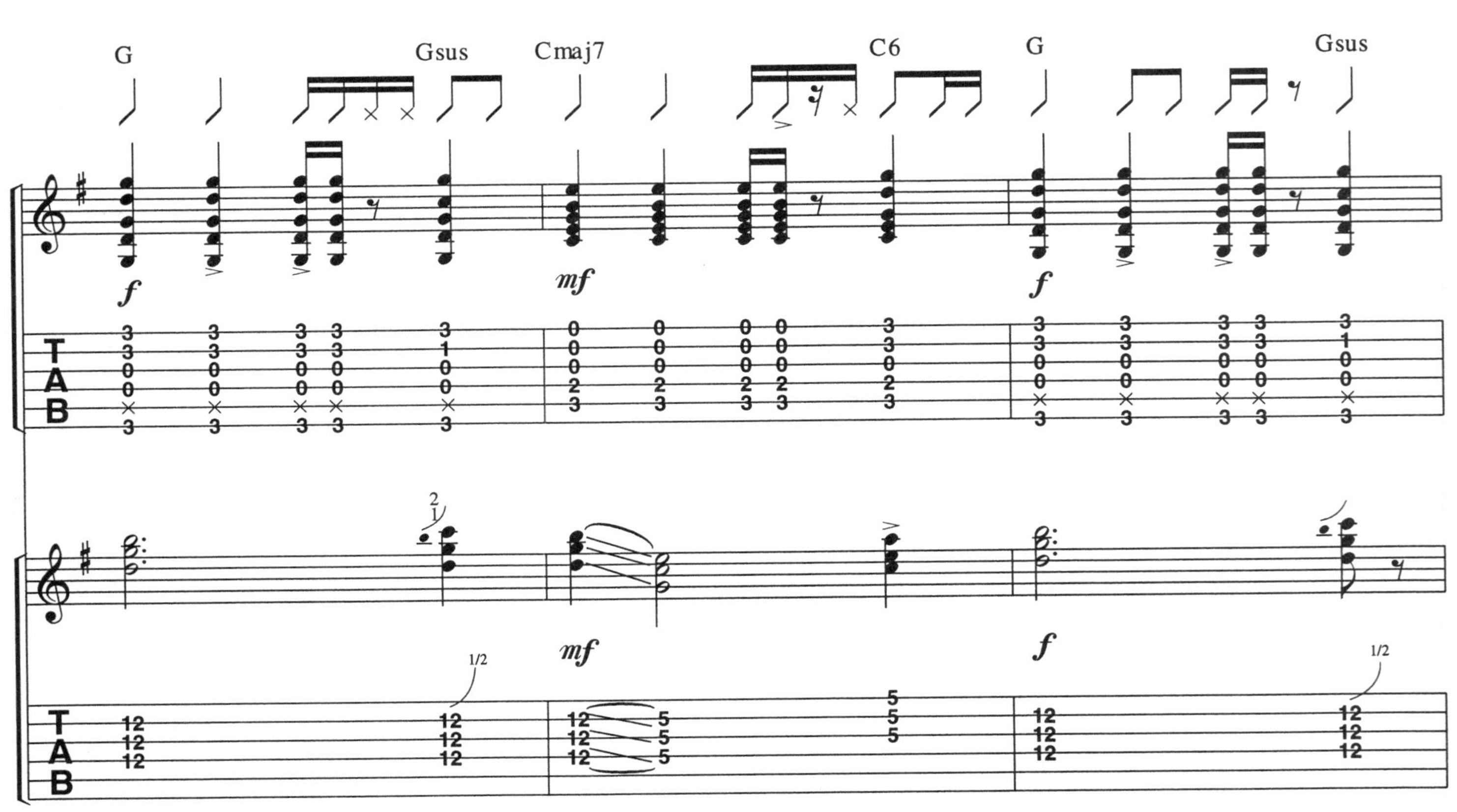
G
Gsus
Cmaj7
C6
G
Gsus
f
mf
f
TAB

*Sul ponticello (microtonal harmonic glissandos: from sliding up and down the strings while tremelo bowing near bridge).
**New chord name derived from Bass guitar part.
***With chorus and tremelo effect set to ♪.

*Arranged one octave lower than recording.

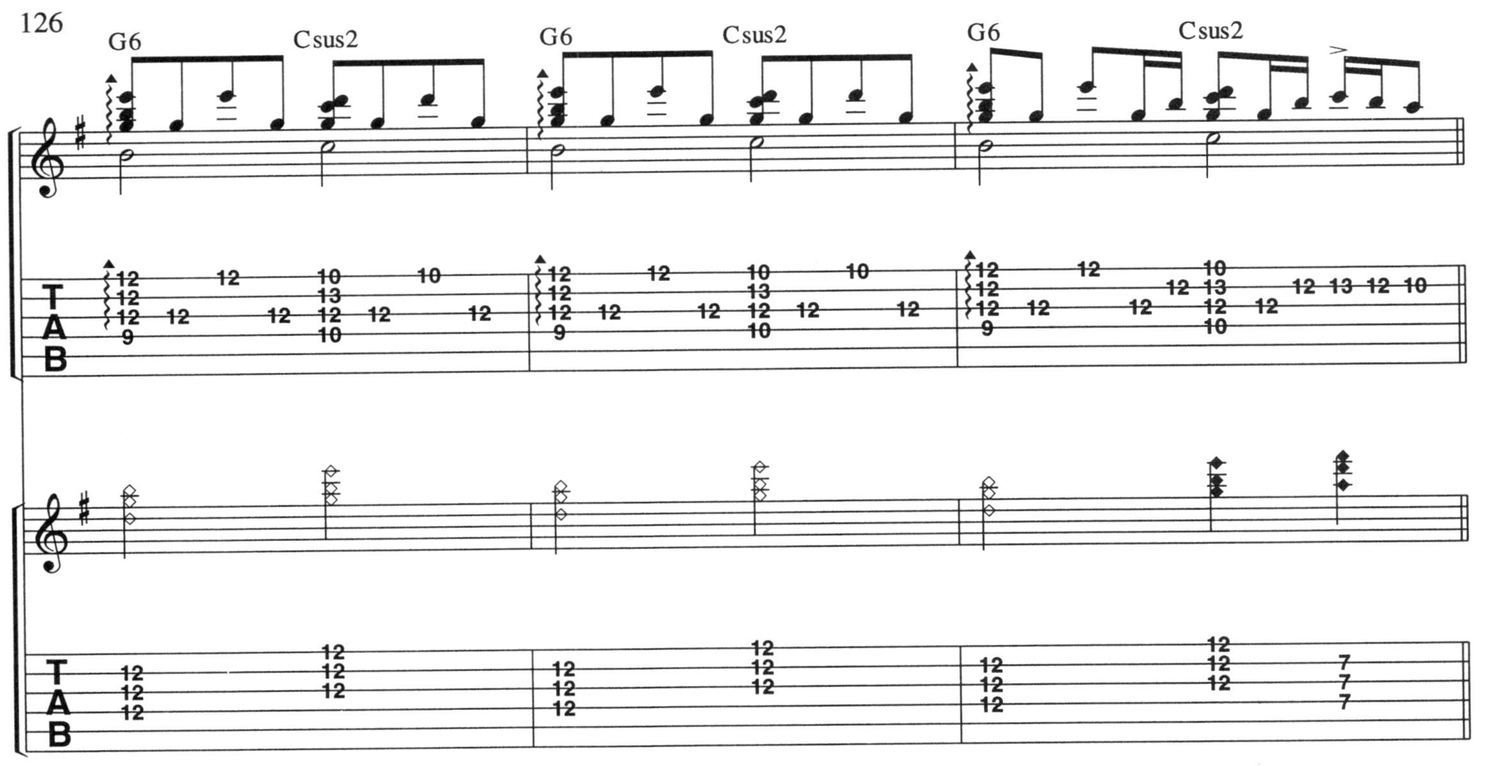

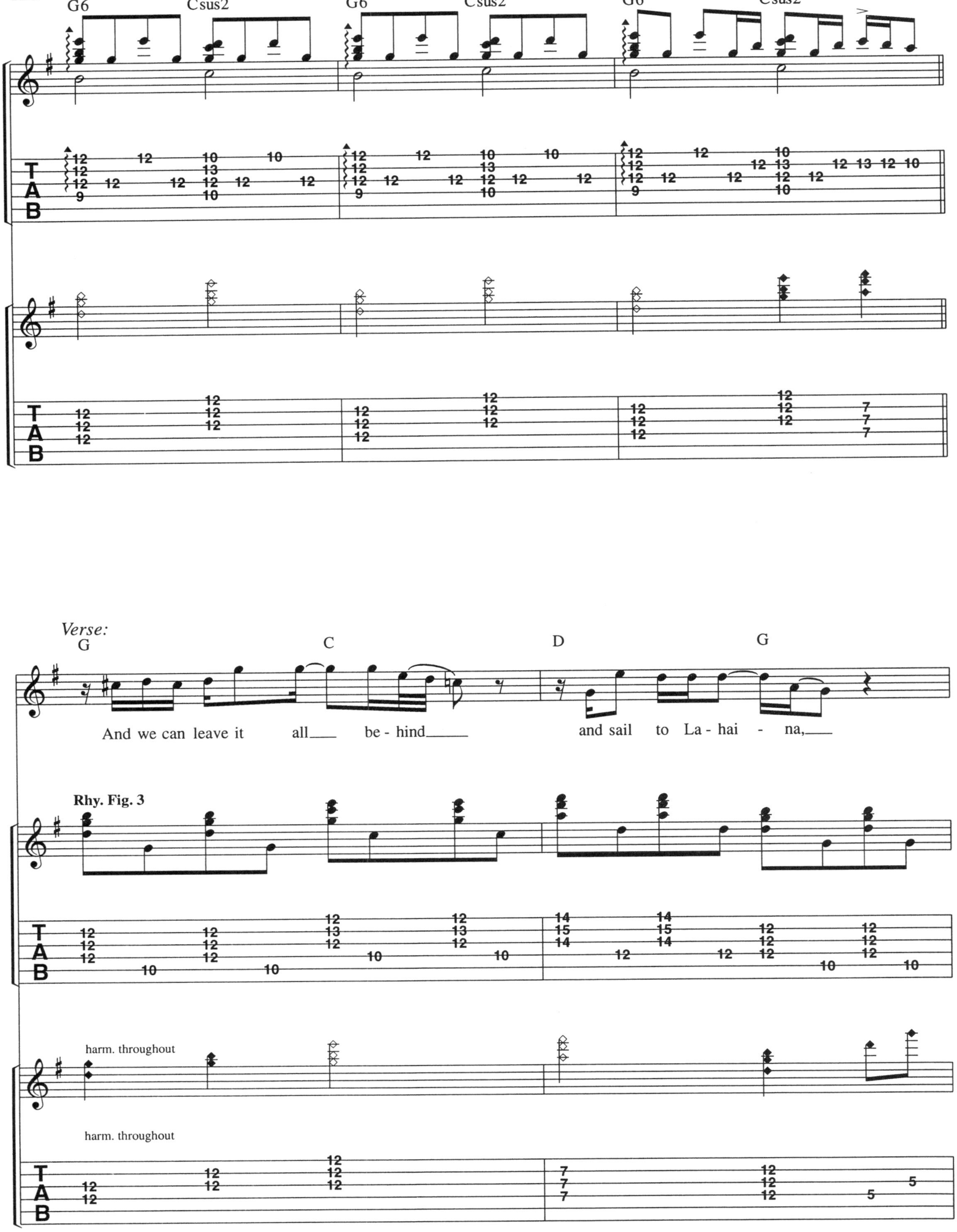

*Verse:*

G C D G

And we can leave it all___ be - hind_____ and sail to La - hai - na,___

**Rhy. Fig. 3**

harm. throughout

harm. throughout

C
D
G
just like the mis-sion - ar - ies__ did__
so__ man-y years a - go.__
C
D
G
They e-ven brought a ne-on sign____ that said, "Je - sus is com - ing."_____

C
D
G
Brought the white man's_ bur - den down,____
brought the white man's reign.__
end Rhy. Fig. 3
Verse:
with Rhy. Fig. 3 cont. simile
G
C
D
G
Gtr. 2
Who will pro- vide the grand_ de- sign?____
What is yours and what is mine?_
Gtr. 3
mf
Gtr. 4
mf

C
D
G
'Cause there is no more_ new_ fron - tier,__
we have__ got to make it here.___
C
D
G
We sat - is - fy our end - less needs__
and just - i - fy our blood - y deeds__

C
D
G
Gsus
in the name of des - ti - ny,
and in the name of God.
Verse:
G
C
D
G
And you can see them there
on Sun-day morn - ing;
Background vocals:
Ah,

C
D
G
they stand up and sing a - bout
what it's like up there.
ah,

G
C
D
G
And they call it par - a - dise, I don't know why.
ah,
T
A
B

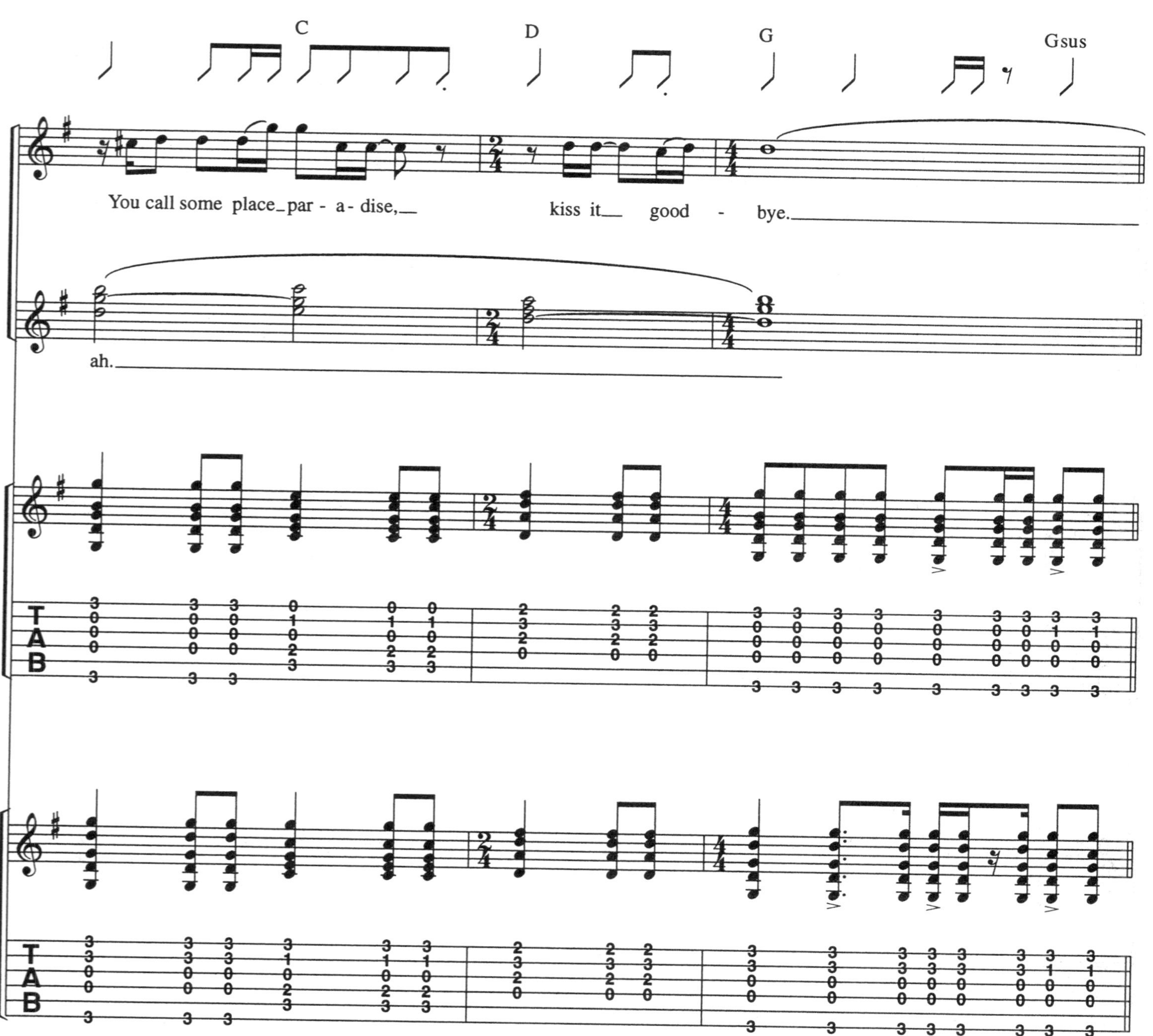
C
D
G
Gsus
You call some place_par - a- dise,_
kiss it_ good - bye._
ah._

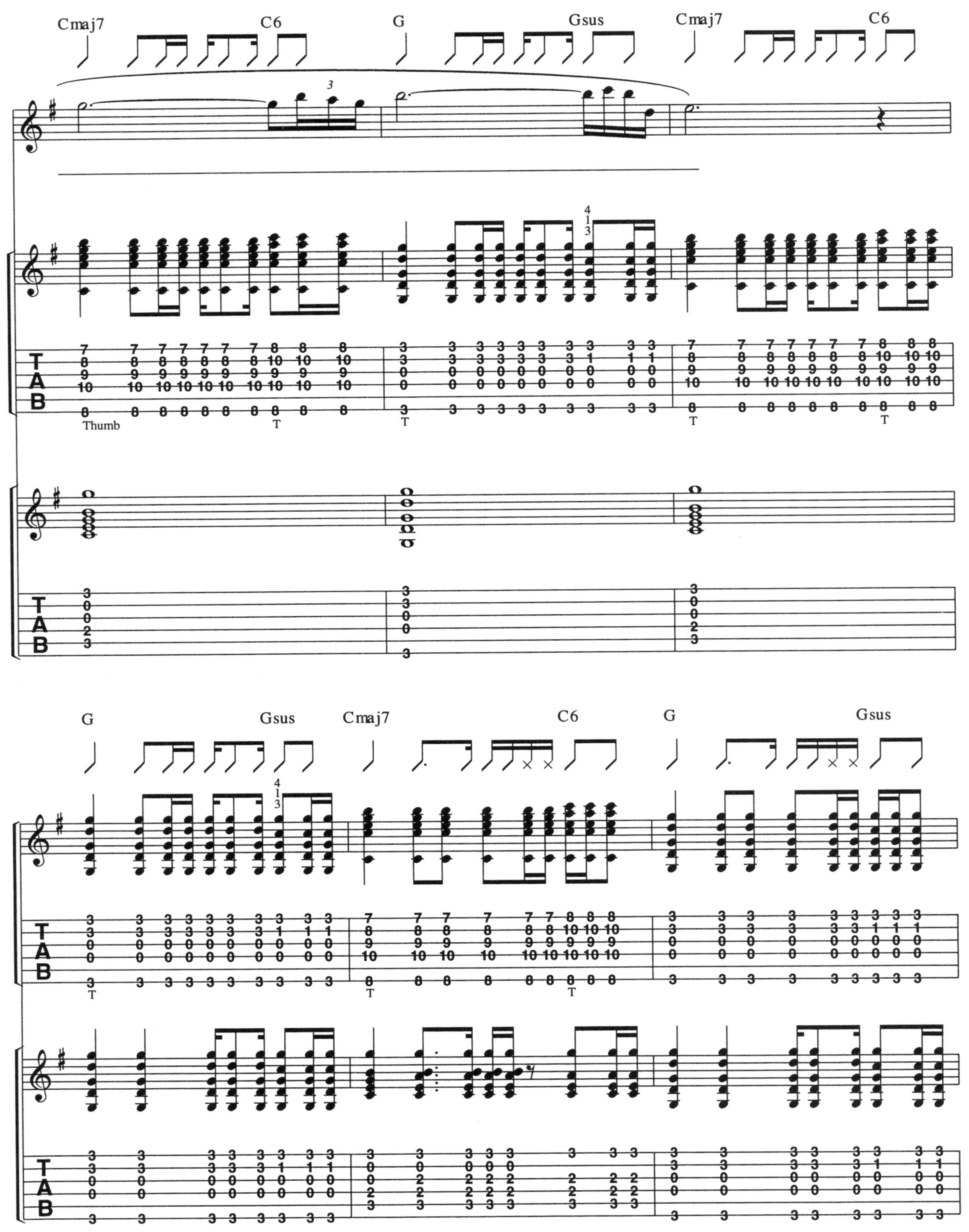

Cmaj7
C6
G
Gsus
Cmaj7
C6
Thumb
G
Gsus
Cmaj7
C6
G
Gsus

Cmaj7
C6
G
Gsus
Cmaj7
C6
Ooh.
G
Gsus
Cmaj7
C6
ooh,
ooh,

*Natural harmonics at XII, strum strings ③ - ①.
**Natural harmonics at V, strum strings ④ - ②.

# take it easy

Words and Music by
JACKSON BROWNE and GLENN FREY

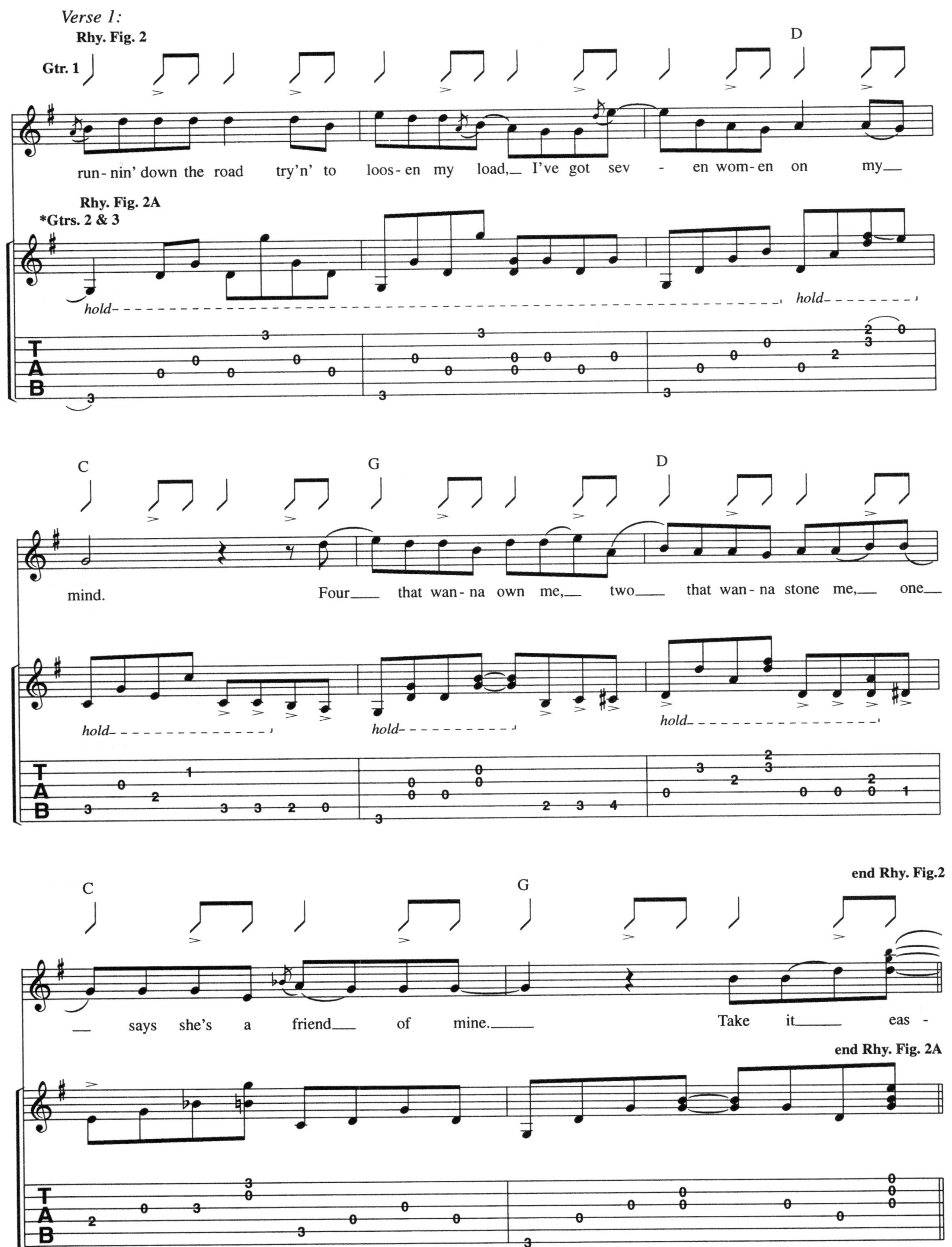
Verse 1:
Rhy. Fig. 2
Gtr. 1
D
run-nin' down the road try'n' to loos-en my load, I've got sev - en wom-en on my
Rhy. Fig. 2A
*Gtrs. 2 & 3
hold
hold
C
G
D
mind. Four that wan-na own me, two that wan-na stone me, one
hold
hold
hold
C
G
end Rhy. Fig.2
says she's a friend of mine. Take it eas -
end Rhy. Fig. 2A

Chorus:
Rhy. Fig. 3
Em
C
y, take it eas -
Rhy. Fig. 3A
hold
hold
hold
G
Am7
G/B
C
D
y. Don't let the sound of your own wheels drive you cra -
(Ooh,
hold
hold
hold
hold
Em
end Rhy. Fig. 3
Rhy. Fig. 4
G/B
C
- zy.
Light - en up while you still can,
ooh.)
end Rhy. Fig 3A
Rhy. Fig. 4A
hold
hold
hold

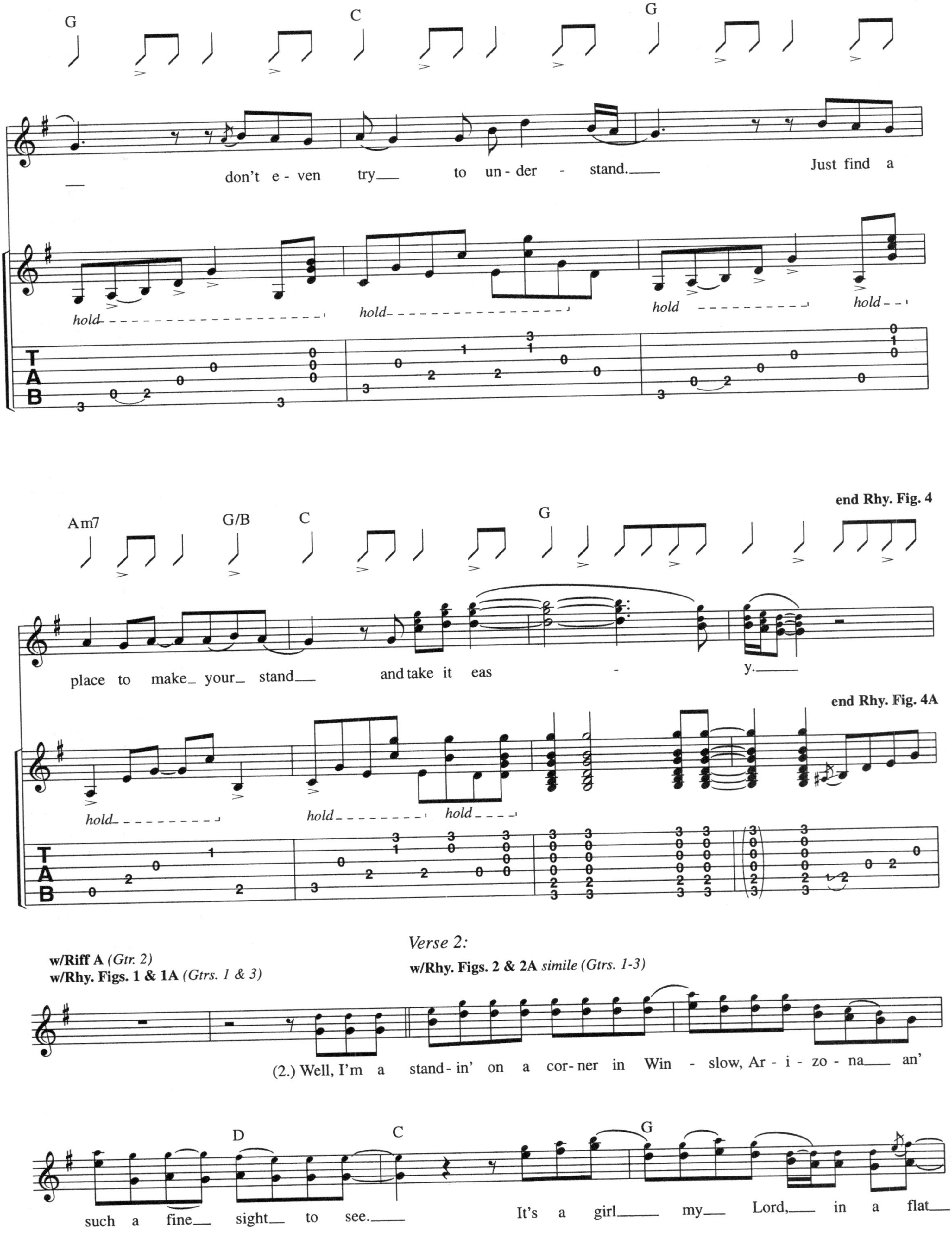

end Rhy. Fig. 4

Am7 G/B C G

place to make your stand and take it eas - y.

end Rhy. Fig. 4A

*hold* *hold* *hold*

TAB

*Verse 2:*

**w/Riff A** *(Gtr. 2)*
**w/Rhy. Figs. 1 & 1A** *(Gtrs. 1 & 3)*

**w/Rhy. Figs. 2 & 2A** *simile (Gtrs. 1-3)*

(2.) Well, I'm a stand - in' on a cor - ner in Win - slow, Ar - i - zo - na an'

D
C
G
— bed Ford___ slow-in' down to take a look at___ me.___ Come on___ ba-
(Ba-
Chorus:
w/Rhy. Figs. 3 & 3A simile (Gtrs. 1-3)
Em
C
G
- by, don't_ say_ may - be, I___ got-ta
- by, may - be.
Am7
G/B
C
D
Em
G/B
know if your_ sweet___ love___ is gon-na save___ me.__ We may lose_
Ooh,___ ooh,___ )
w/Rhy. Figs. 4 & 4A simile (Gtrs. 1-3)
C
G
C
G
— and we may___ win, though we will nev-er be here_ a-gain.___ So o-pen
Am7
G/B
C
G
up, I'm climb-in' in,___ so take it eas - y.___
(All_ right!)
Guitar Solo:
w/Rhy. Figs. 2 & 2A simile (Gtrs. 1 & 3)
Gtr. 2
f hold bend
D
C
G
D
C
G
hold
w/Rhy. Figs. 3 & 3A simile (Gtrs. 1 & 3)
Em

Gtrs. 1 and 3 subst. w/Rhy. Fill 1
D
C
G
Am7
G/B
C
D
hold
Gtrs. 1 & 3 subst. w/Rhy. Fill 2
Em
D
(3.) Well, I'm
Verse 3:
w/Rhy. Figs. 2 & 2A simile (Gtrs. 1-3)
G
D
Gtrs. 1-3 subst. w/Rhy. Fill 3
Am7
run-nin' down the road try'n' to loos-en my load, got a world of trou-ble on my mind. Look-
(Ooh, ooh, ooh, ooh.
Rhy. Fill 1
D
Gtr. 1
Gtr. 3
hold
Rhy. Fill 2
Em
D
Gtr. 1
Gtr. 3
hold
Rhy. Fill 3
Am7
Gtr. 1
Gtrs. 2 & 3
hold

G D C
- in' for a lov - er who won't blow my cov - er, she's so hard to find.
Ooh, ooo, ooh,
Chorus:
w/Rhy. Figs. 3 & 3A simile (Gtrs. 1-3)
G Em
Take it eas - y, take it eas -
ooh.)
C G Am7 G/B C D
- y. Don't let the sound of them own wheels drive you
(Ooh,
w/Rhy. Figs. 4 & 4A simile, Gtrs. 1-3 (1st 5 bars only)
Em G/B C G
cra - zy. Come on ba - by, don't say may-
Ba - by, may-
C G Am7 G/B
- be, I got - ta know if your sweet
- be. Ooh,
C G
Gtr. 1
love is gon - na save me.
save me.)
Gtrs. 2 & 3
hold

*Outro:*

**2nd time subst. w/Rhy. Fill 4** *(Gtr. 2 only)*

**Rhy. Fig. 5**

C G

Ooh, ooh, ooh, ooh.

**Rhy. Fig. 5A**

*hold hold hold hold hold hold hold*

TAB

**w/Rhy. Figs. 5 & 5A** *simile, (Gtrs. 1-3)*

**1st time subst. w/Rhy. Fill 5** *(Gtr. 2 only)*

C G

Ooh, ooh, ooh, ooh.

**w/Rhy. Figs. 5 & 5A** *simile, Gtrs. 1 & 3 (6 times)*

***Gtr. 2** C

TAB

*Slightly overdriven.

G

*T

TAB

*Fret w/thumb and slide.

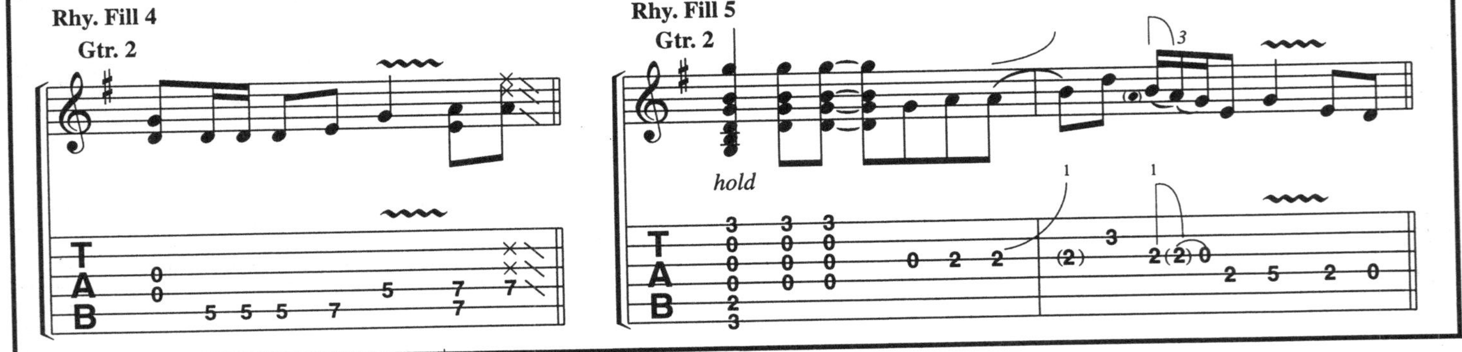

C
G
C
G
C
hold
G
hold
hold
8va

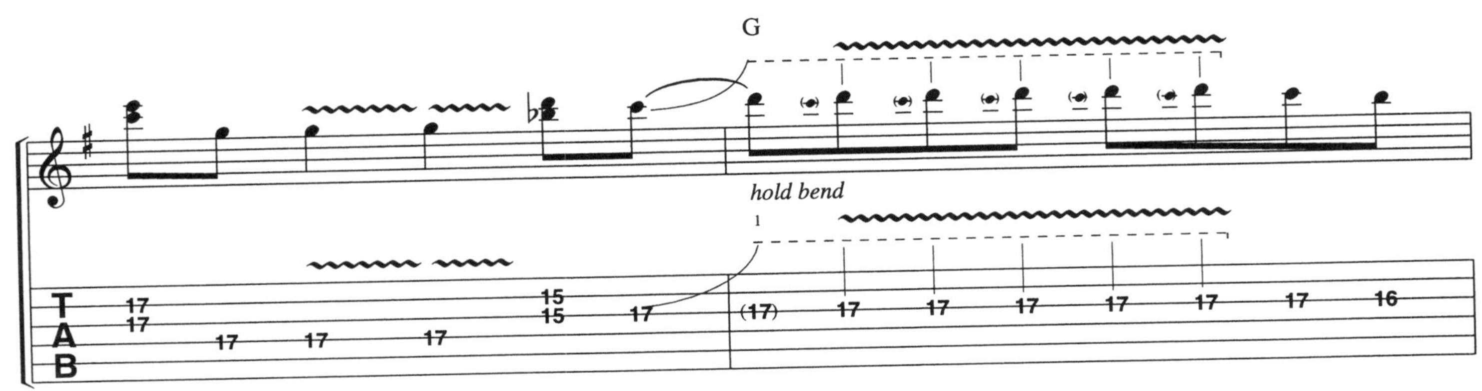


**w/1st 2 bars of Rhy. Figs. 5 & 5A** *simile (Gtrs. 1 & 3)*

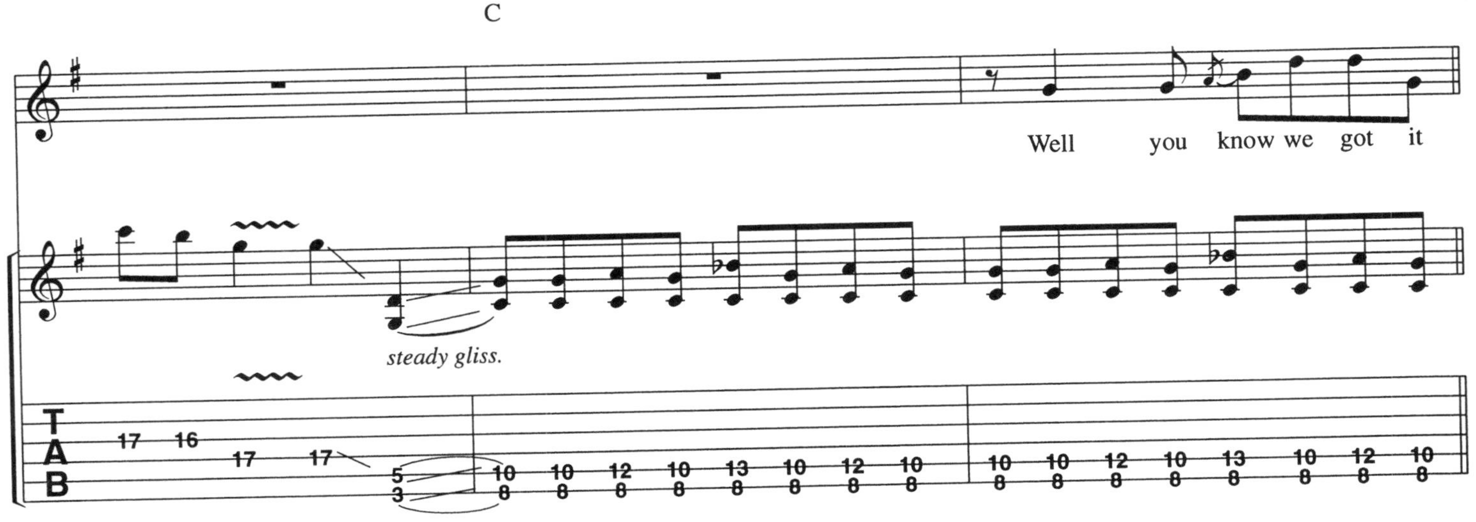

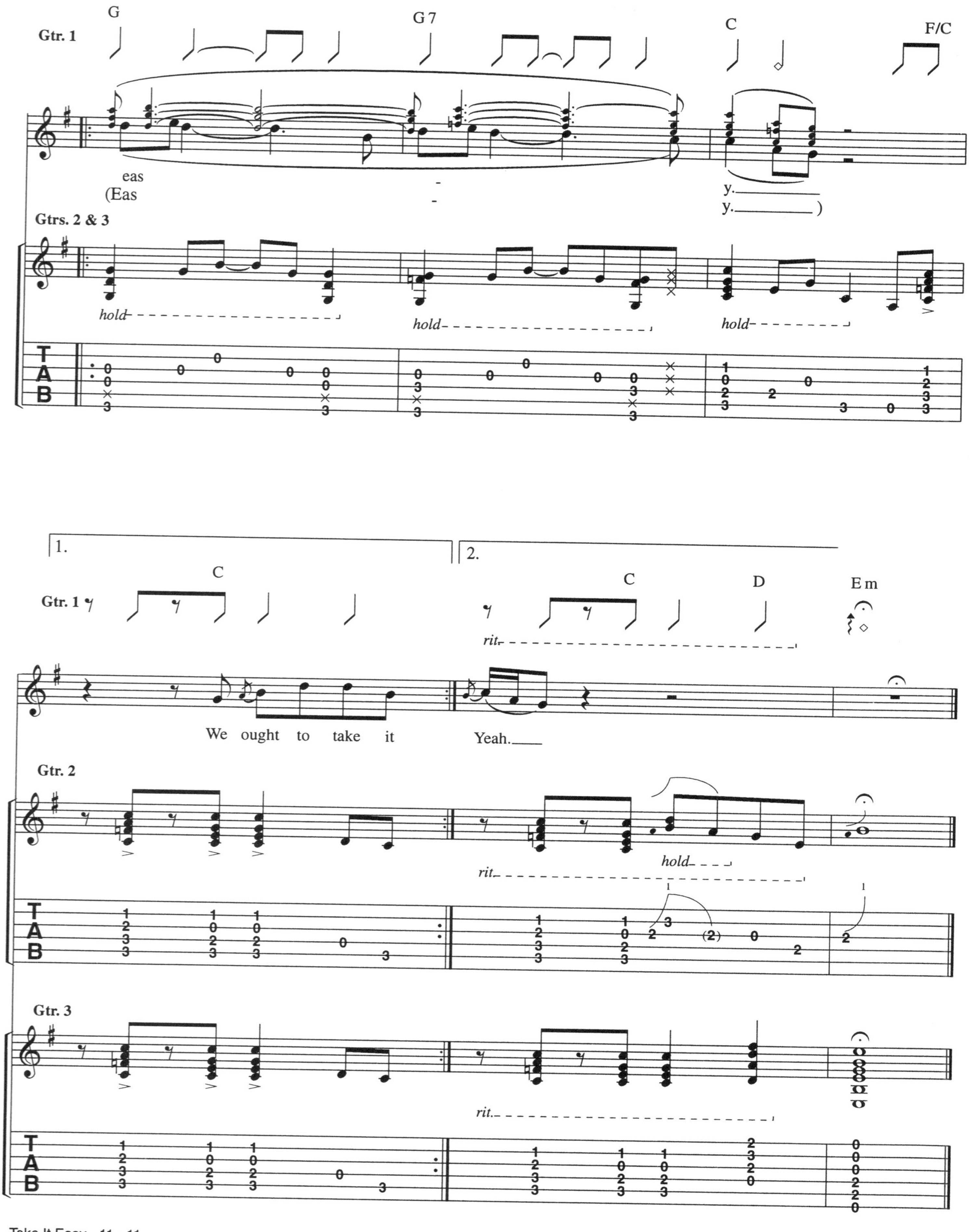

1.
2.

C
C
D
Em

Gtr. 1

rit.

We ought to take it
Yeah.

Gtr. 2

hold
rit.

Gtr. 3

rit.

# in the city

Words and Music by
JOE WALSH and BARRY DeVORZON

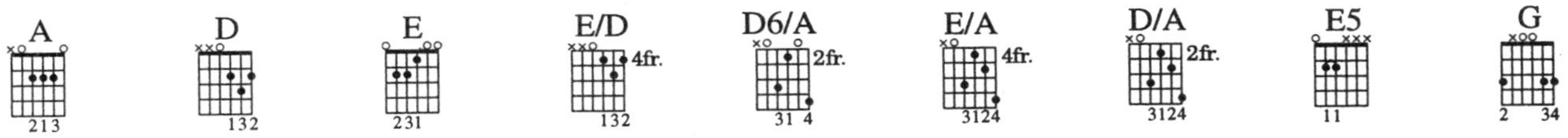
Gtrs. 2&3
A
D
E
E/D
4fr.
D6/A
2fr.
E/A
4fr.
D/A
2fr.
E5
G

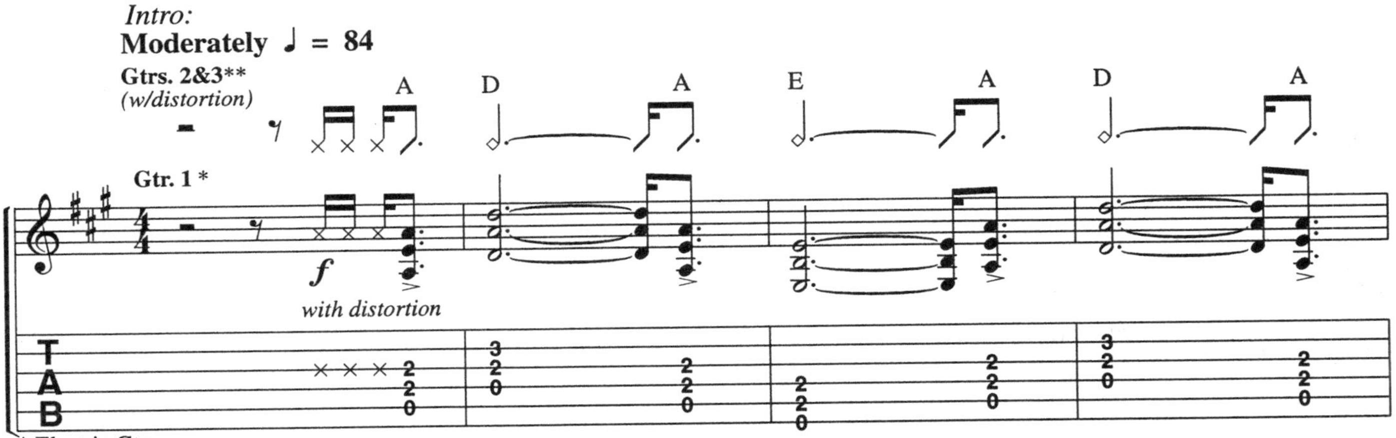
Intro:
Moderately ♩ = 84
Gtrs. 2&3**
(w/distortion)
A D A E A D A
Gtr. 1 *
f
with distortion
TAB

* Electric Gtr.
**Electric Gtrs. arranged as one (Gtr. 2 plays lower 3 strings of each chord only; "power chords", similar to Gtr. 1.)

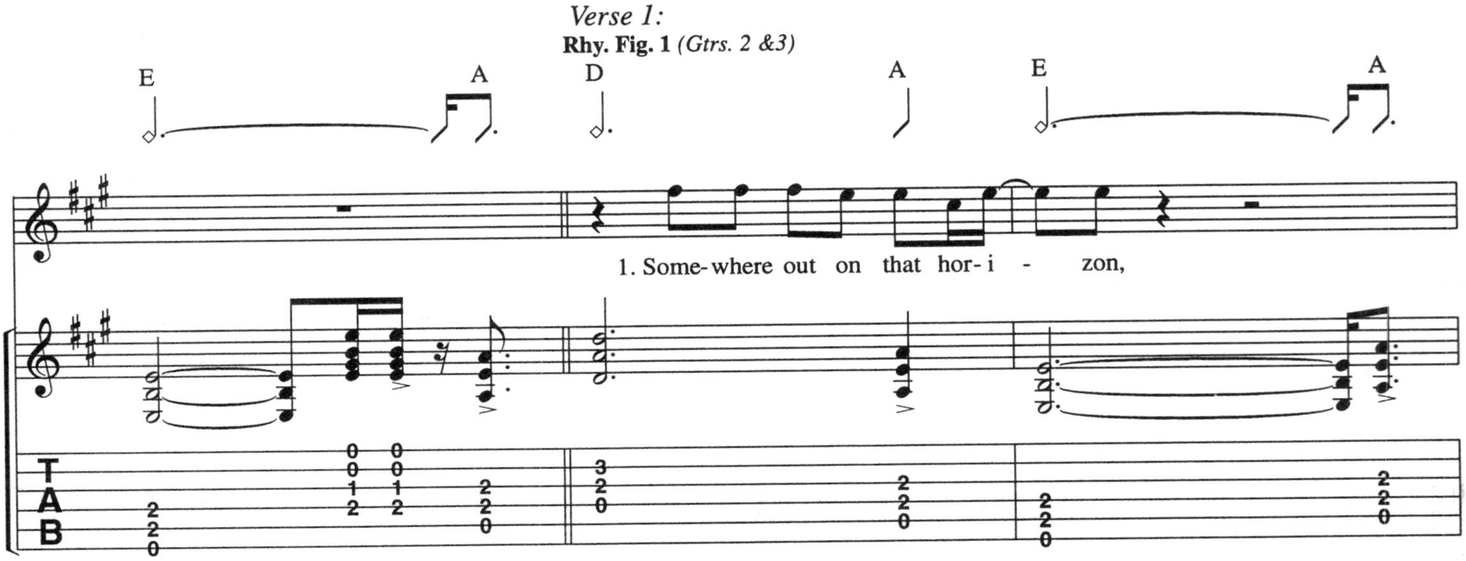
Verse 1:
Rhy. Fig. 1 (Gtrs. 2 &3)
E A D A E A
1. Some-where out on that hor-i - zon,
TAB

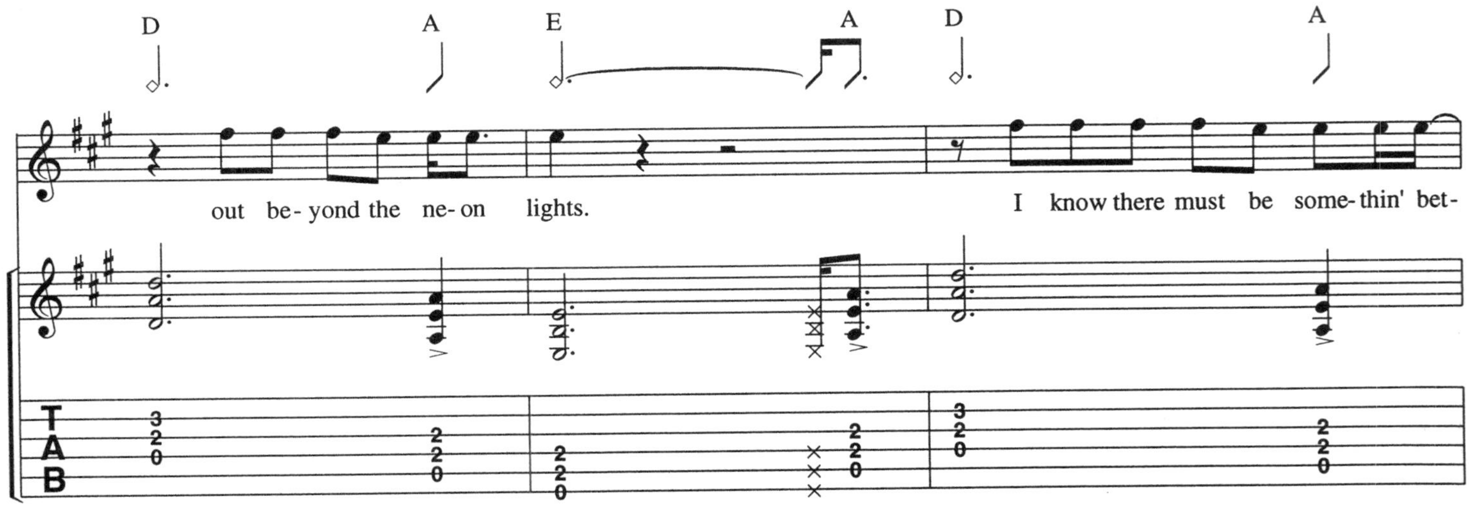
D A E A D A
out be-yond the ne-on lights.
I know there must be some-thin' bet-
TAB

E A D E/D A end Rhy. Fig. 2 E
- ter, but there's no-where else in sight.
Verse 2:
with Rhy Fig. 1 Cont. simile
D A E A D A
It's sur-viv-al in the cit-y child-ren, when you live from day to day.
Background vocals:
Ooh, Ooh,
E A D A E A D E/D
City streets don't have much pit-y, no. When you're down that's where you'll
ooh. ooh, ooh,

Chorus:
Rhy. Fig 2 (Gtr. 3)
Gtr. 3
A
D6/A
E/A
stay.
ooh.
In the
cit - y,
Uh -
Rhy. Fig. 2A (Gtrs. 1 & 2)
Gtrs. 1 & 2
* Three voice unison.
D/A
A
huh.
Ooh,
ooh.
end Rhy. Fig.2
D6/A
E/A
D/A
E5
In the
cit - y,
uh - huh.
end Rhy. Fig. 2A
* Three voice unison.

Guitar Solo:
**Gtrs 2&3
Gtr. 1
8va *
pick slide
with slide throughout
* Slide from bridge to second fret.
** Arranged as before in verses.
*** Echo effect this note only.
* Echo effect.
** Begin slide on beat two.
Verse 3:
with Rhy. Fig. 1 cont. simile
3. I was born here in the cit - y,
with my back a-gainst the wall.
Noth-ing grows and life ain't ver- y pret- ty;
no one's there to catch you when you fall.
4. Oh,

Verse 4:
with Rhy Fig. 1 cont. simile:
D A E A D A E A
it's some-where out on that hor-i-zon, a-way from the ne-on sky.
Background vocals:
Ooh. ooh, ooh,
Gtr. 1
*Emphasize third string.
D A E A D E/D
I know there must be some-thing, must be some-thin' bet-ter. I can't stay a-noth-er
ooh, ooh,
Chorus:
with Rhy. Figs. 2&3 cont. simile:
A D/A E/A D/A
night. A-noth-er
ooh. In the cit-y, Uh-huh. Ooh,
* Three voice unison.
A D/A E/A D/A
night. A-noth-er
ooh. In the cit-y, uh-huh.
* Three voice unison.

*Chorus:*
**with Rhy. Fig. 2** *cont. simile:*

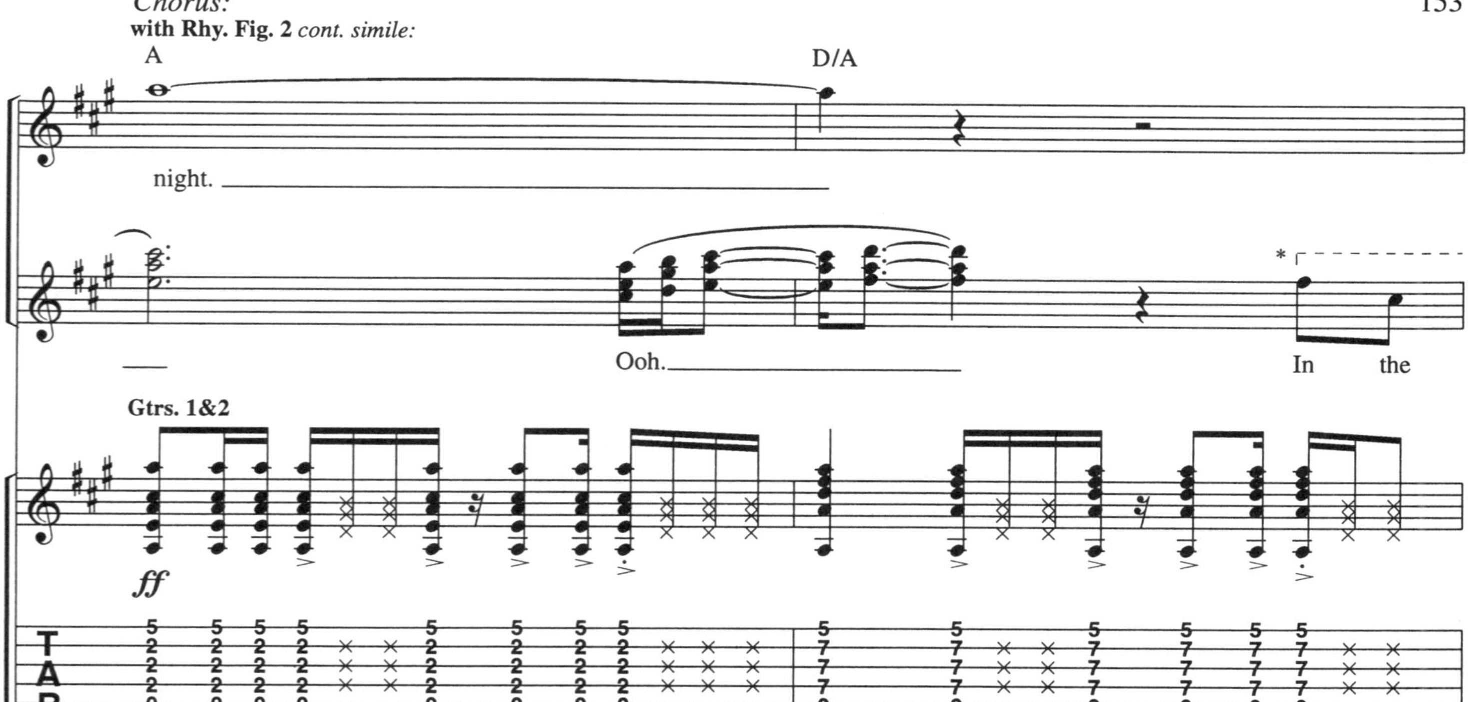


* Three voice unison.

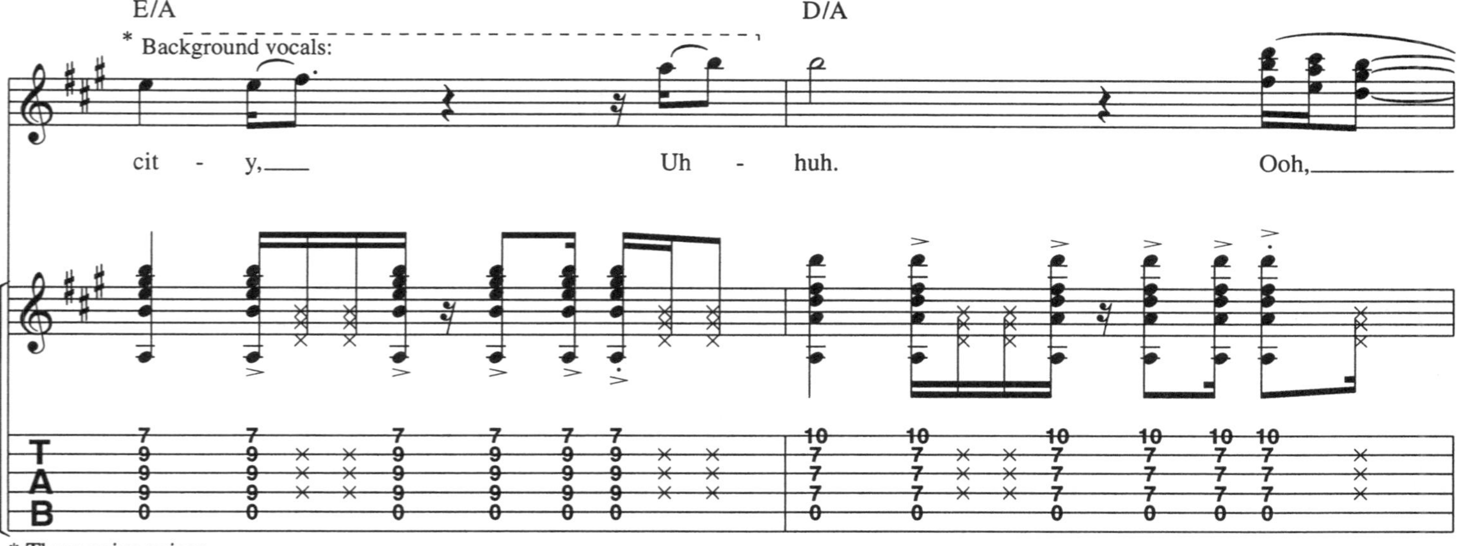


* Three voice unison.

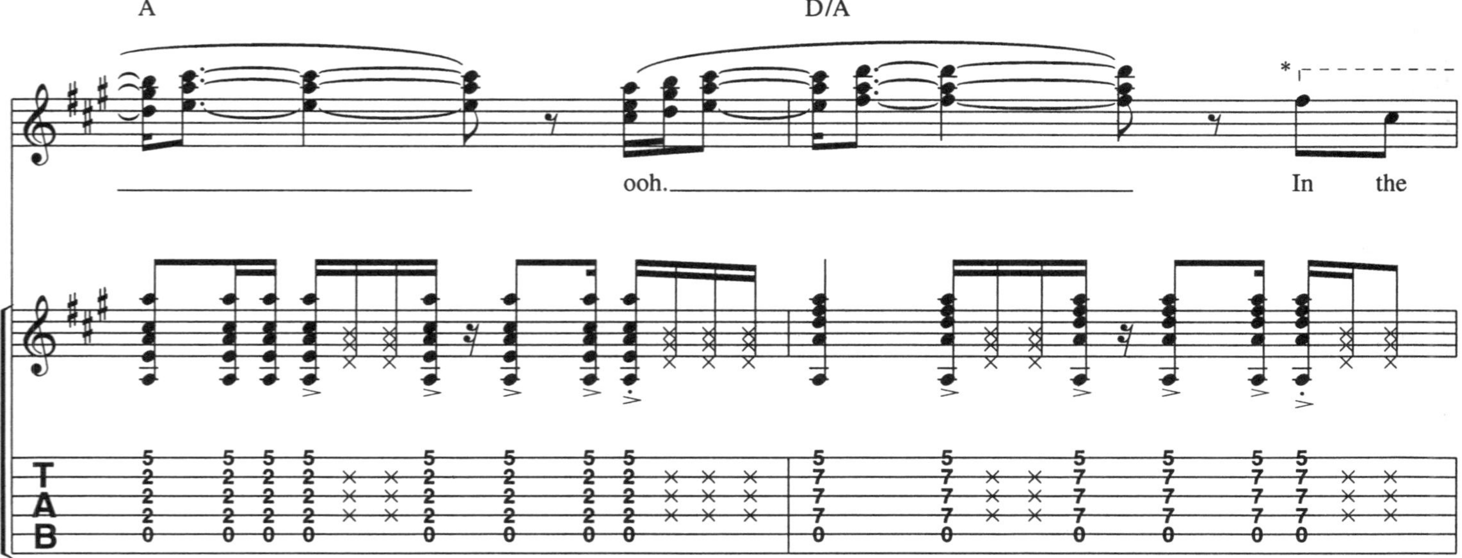


* Three voice unison.

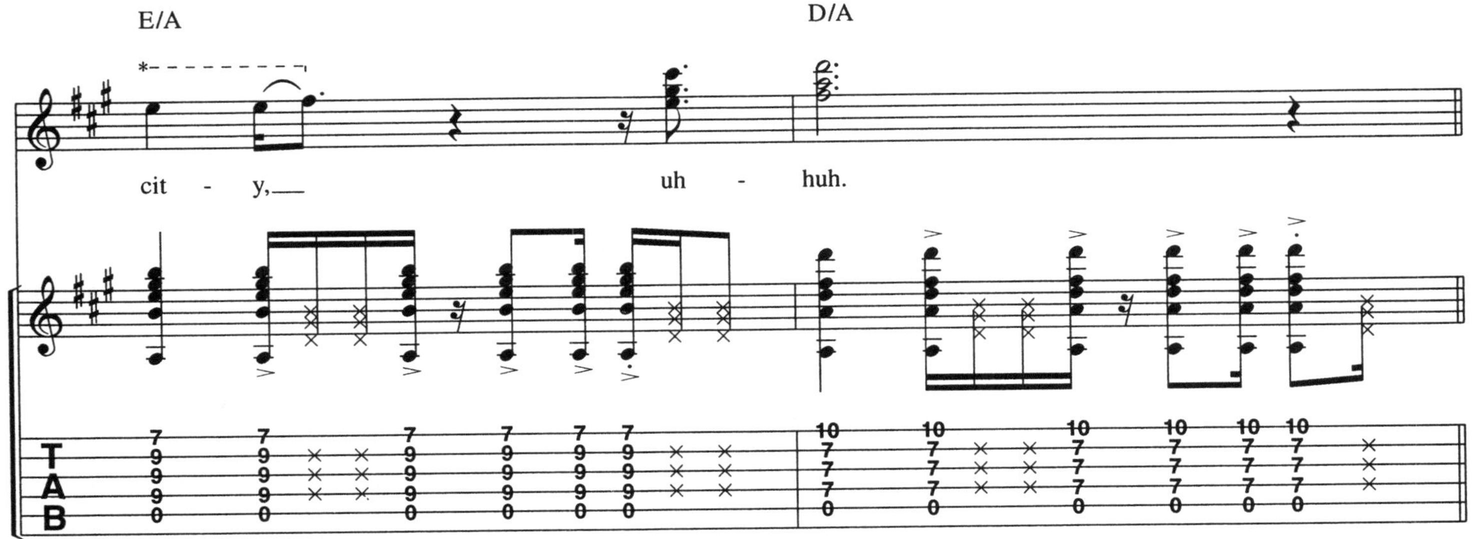


* Three voice unison.

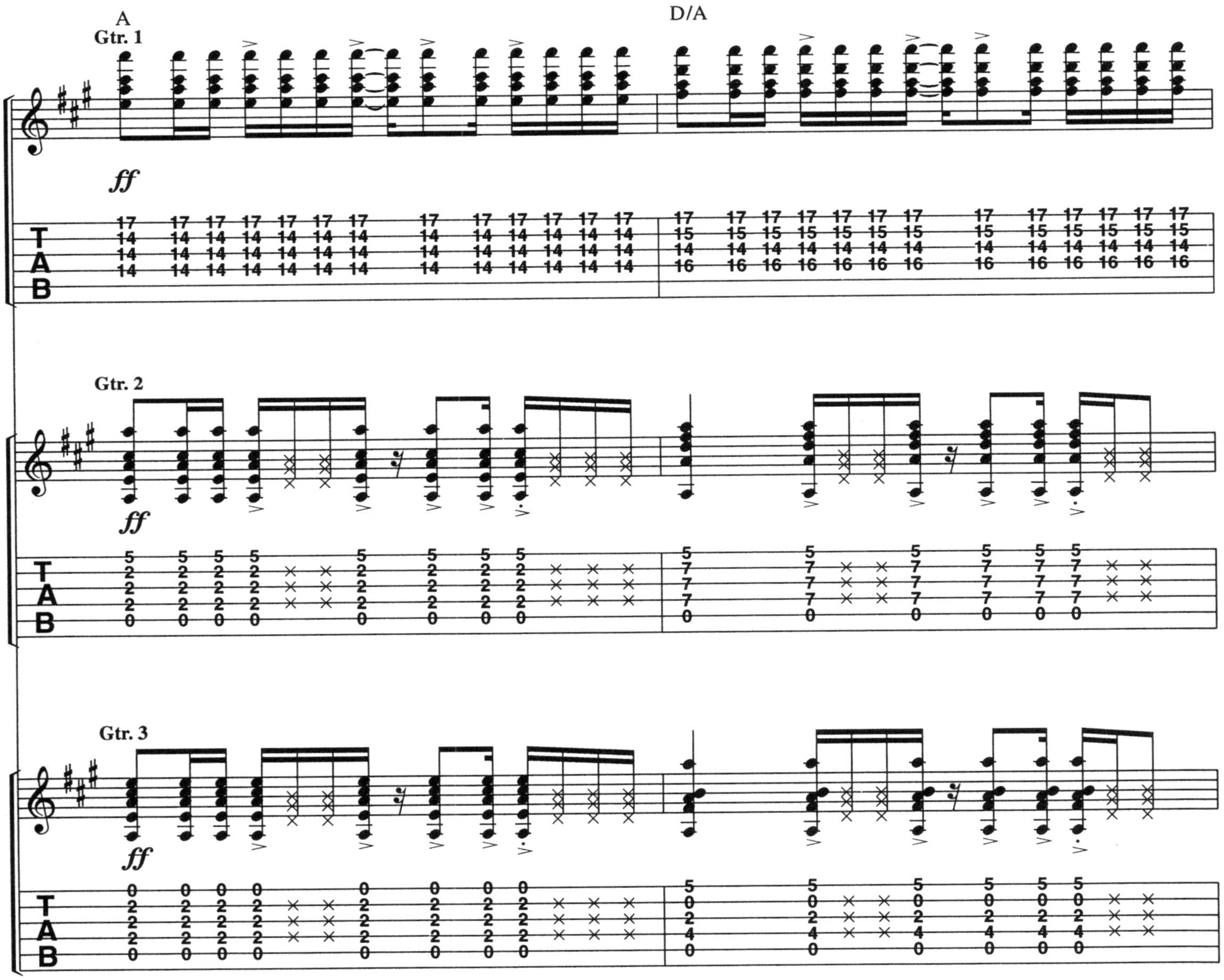

A

D/A

Gtr. 1

*ff*

TAB

Gtr. 2

*ff*

TAB

Gtr. 3

*ff*

TAB

E/A

D/A

A

D/A

E/A D/A

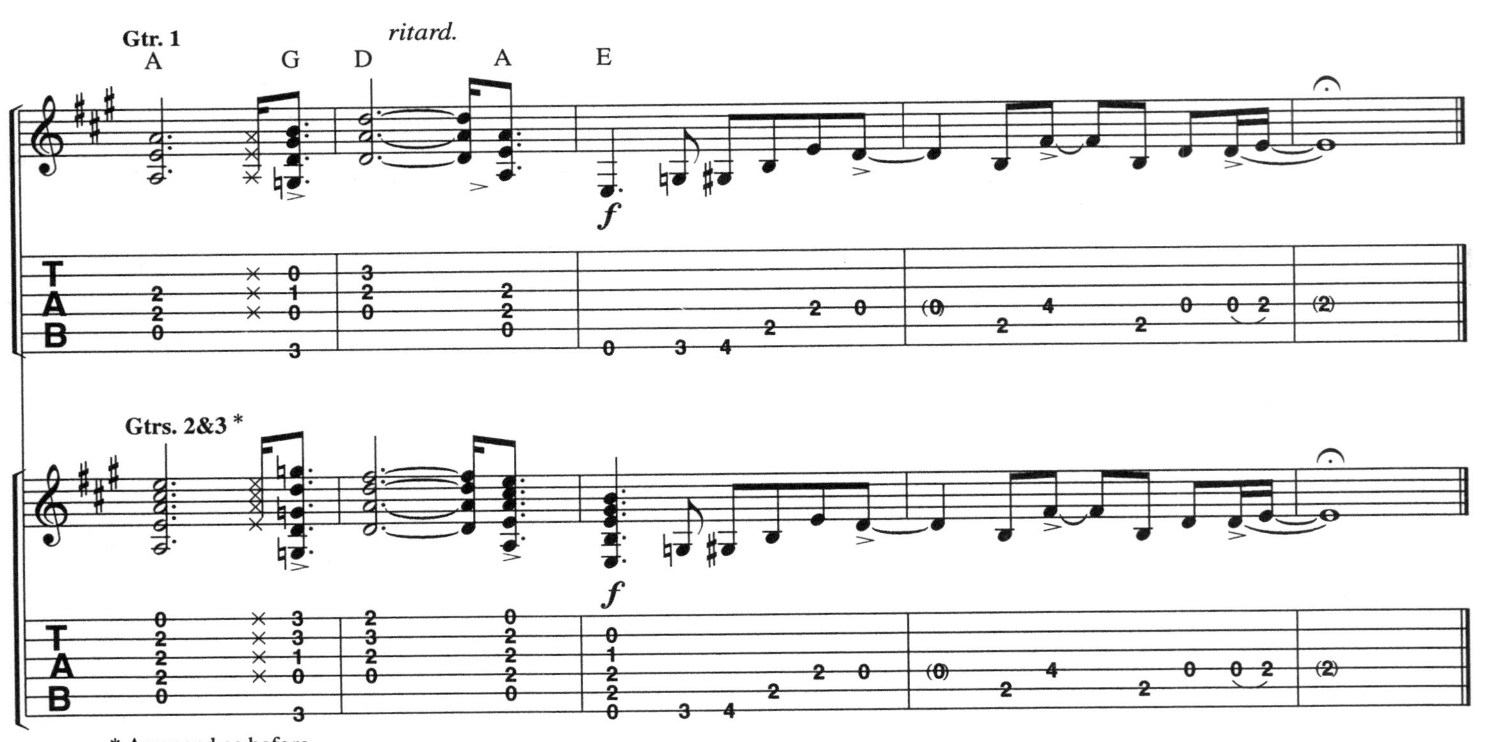


* Arranged as before.

# life in the fast lane

Words and Music by
DON HENLEY, GLENN FREY and JOE WALSH

end Rhy. Fig. 1

⑥ 3fr. 5fr. 6fr. 7fr.
G A A♯ B

end Riff A

end Riff A1

Rhy. Fig. 2

D♯5 E5

Rhy. Fig. 2A

P.M. P.M.

end Rhy. Fig. 2
1. He was a
T
A
B
end Rhy. Fig. 2A
P.M.
Verses 1-3:
Rhy. Fig. 3
E5
hard head - ed man, he was bru - tal - ly hand- some y'all.
2.3. See additional lyrics
Rhy. Fig. 3A

2nd time Gtr. 1 subst. w/Fill 1
3rd time Gtr. 1 subst. w/ Fill 3
end Rhy. Fig. 3
And she was ter - mi - nal - ly pret - ty.
end Rhy. Fig 3A
w/Rhy. Figs. 3 & 3A (Gtrs. 2 & 3)
E5
She held him up and he held her for ran - som in the heart
Gtr. 1
Fill 1
Gtr. 1
Fill 3
Gtr. 1
grad. bend

of the cold, cold city.
He had a
T
A
B
21
1 2 0 2 4 2

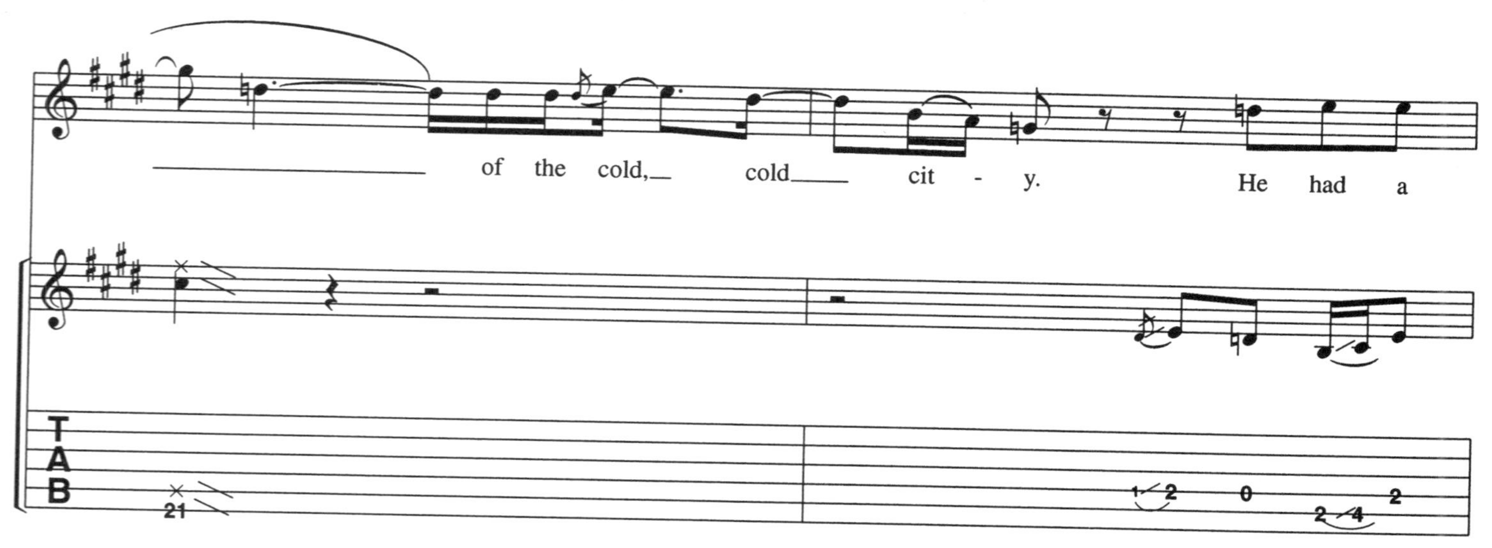

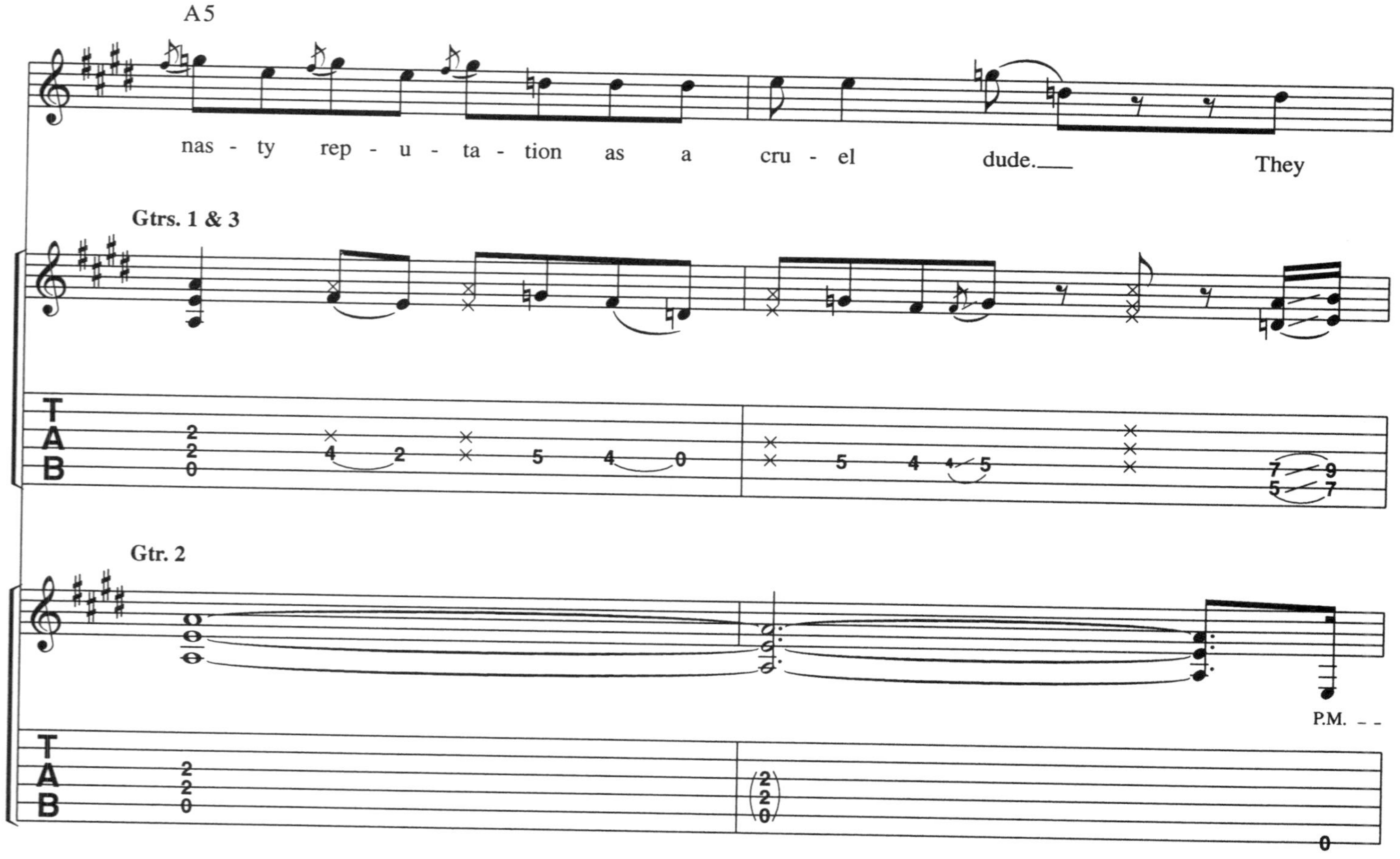

A5
nas - ty rep - u - ta - tion as a cru - el dude.
They
Gtrs. 1 & 3
T
A
B
Gtr. 2
P.M.

E5
said he was ruth - less, they said he was crude. They had
w/slight P.M.
P.M.
P.M.
2nd time Gtr. 2 subst. w/Fill 2
B5
one thing in com - mon, they were good in bed. And she say,
Fill 2
Gtr. 2
pick sl.

2nd time Gtr. 1 subst. w/Fill 4
A 7
Dsus/A
A 7
"Fast - er, fast - er! The lights are turn - in' red."
hold
hold
Chorus:
w/Riffs A &A1 (Gtrs. 1 & 2)
w/Rhy. Fig. 1 (Gtr. 3)
E5
Life in the fast lane,
Sure - ly make you lose your mind.
1.
Life in the fast lane.
w/Rhy. Figs. 2 & 2A (Gtrs. 2 & 3)
Fill 4
Gtr. 1
harm.
harm.
harm.
harm.

2.
Gtr. 3
E5
Yeah.
Gtr. 1
hold
Gtr. 2
Life in the fast lane, ev - 'ry - thing all the time.

To Coda
Cont. in notation
A♯5
Life in the fast lane. Yeah, yeah.
Guitar Solo:
Gtr. 1
B5
w/slight P.M.
Gtr. 2
Gtr. 3
w/slight P.M.

D5
1
½
½
B5
w/slight P.M.
hold
1
½
1
½
1
1
w/slight P.M.

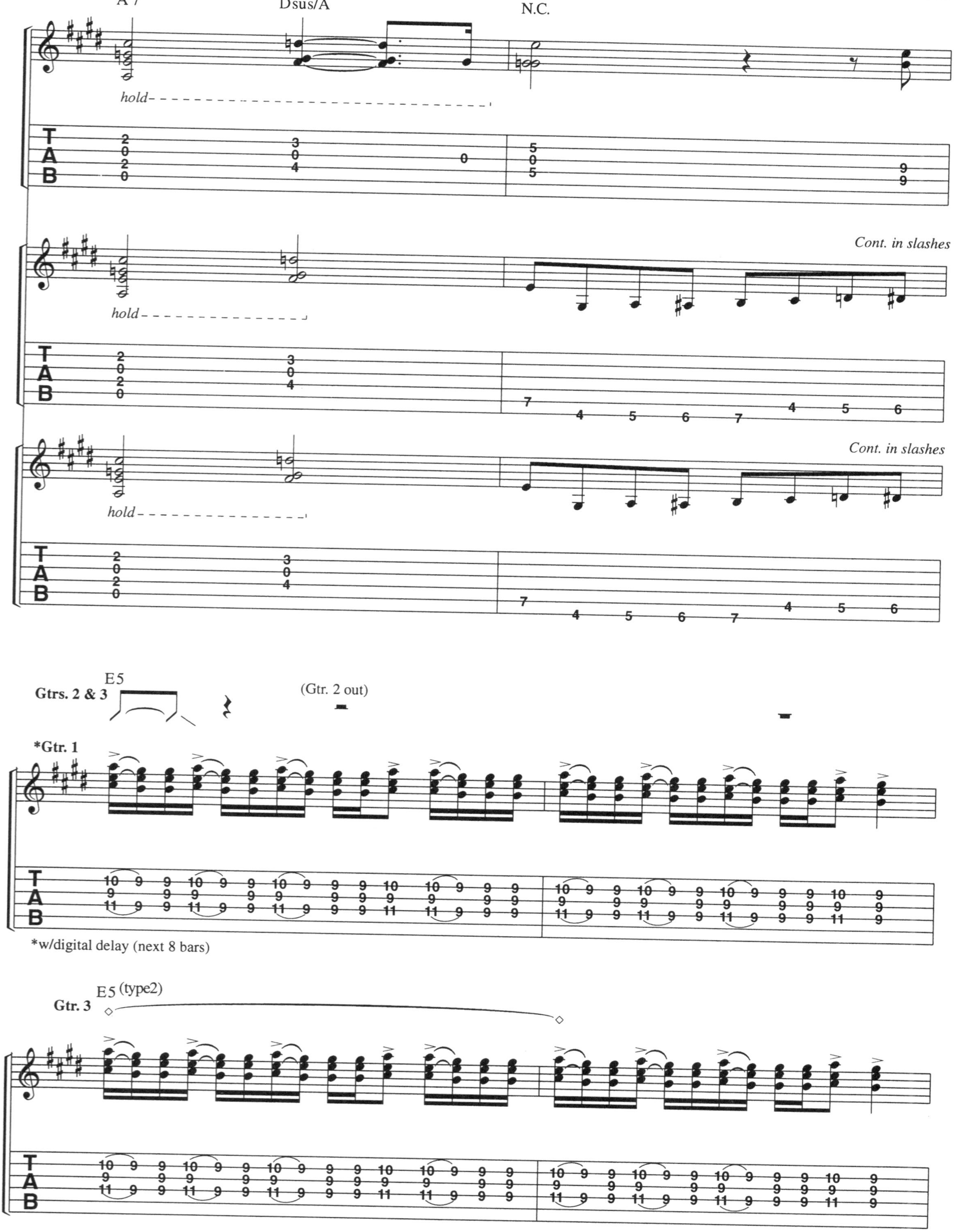

A 7
Dsus/A
N.C.
hold
Cont. in slashes
hold
Cont. in slashes
hold
E5
Gtrs. 2 & 3
(Gtr. 2 out)
*Gtr. 1
*w/digital delay (next 8 bars)
E5 (type2)
Gtr. 3

*D.S. 𝄋 al Coda*
*(take 2nd ending)*

E5

*hold*

Coda
E5
Gtr. 3
Out-Chorus:
E5
yeah.
Life in the fast
Gtr. 1
mf
Gtr. 2
D5
lane.

C5
Life in the fast lane.
A5
Mmm hmm.

*Outro Solo:*

**w/Rhy. Figs. 2 & 2A,** *Gtrs. 2 & 3 (2 times)*

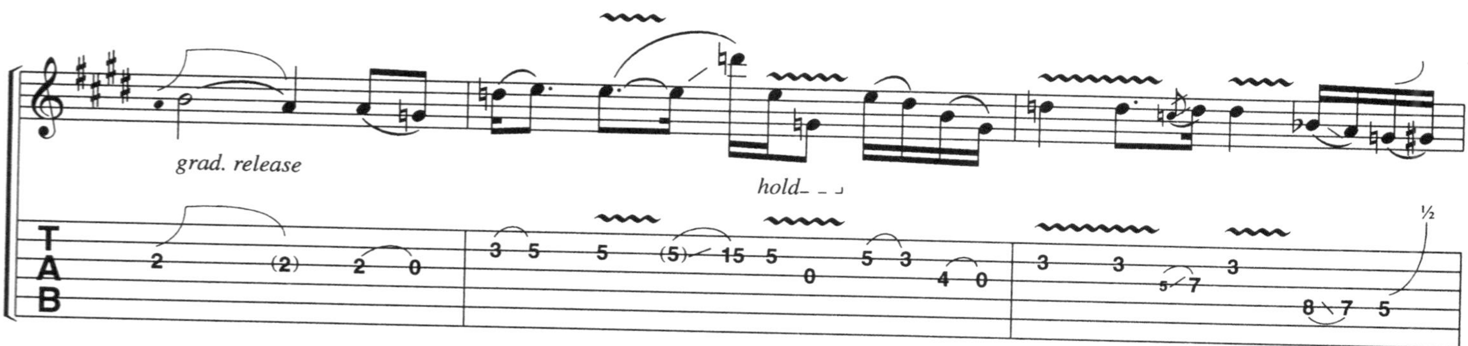

**w/Rhy. Fig. 2A** *simile, Gtr. 2 (2 times)*

*w/digital delay until end

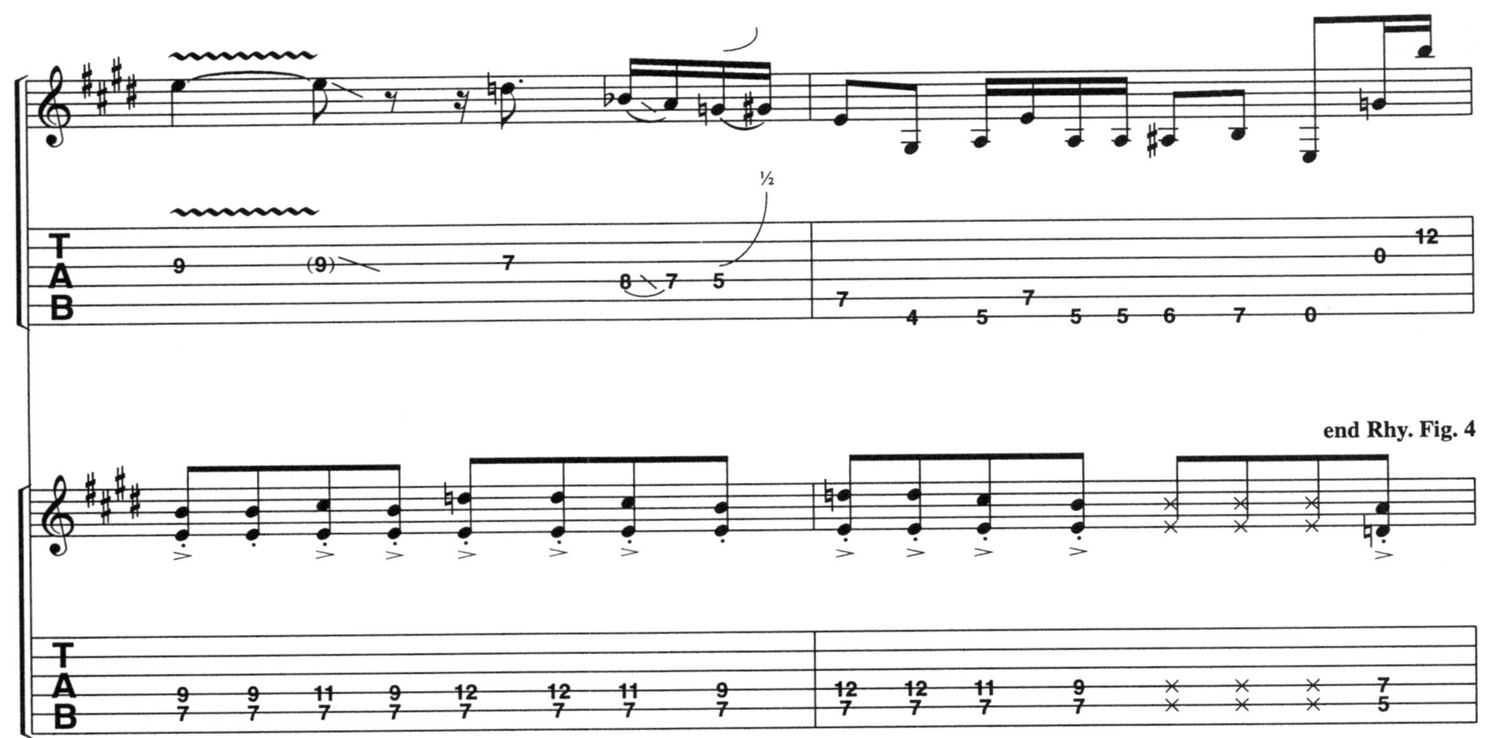


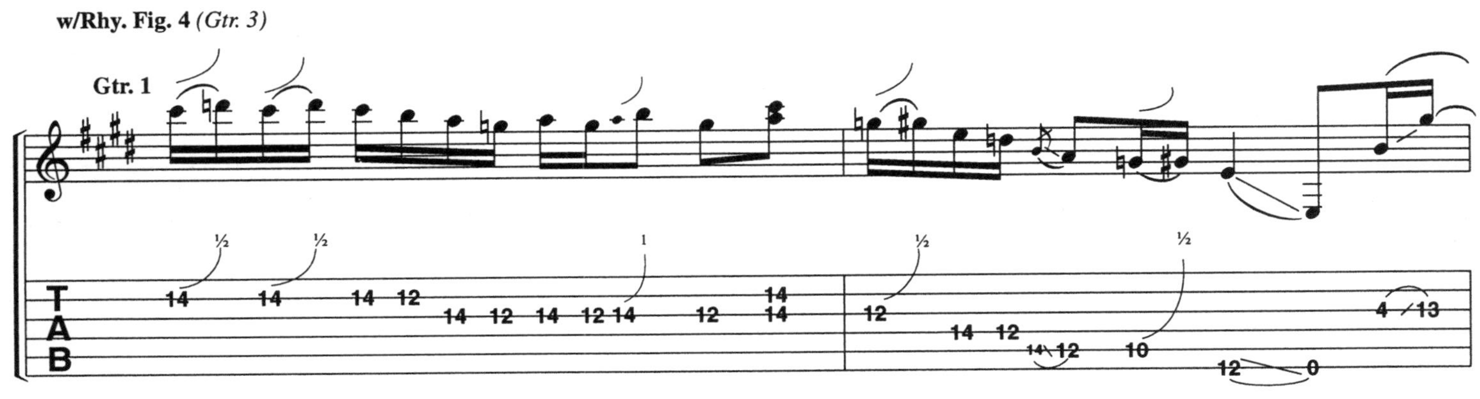


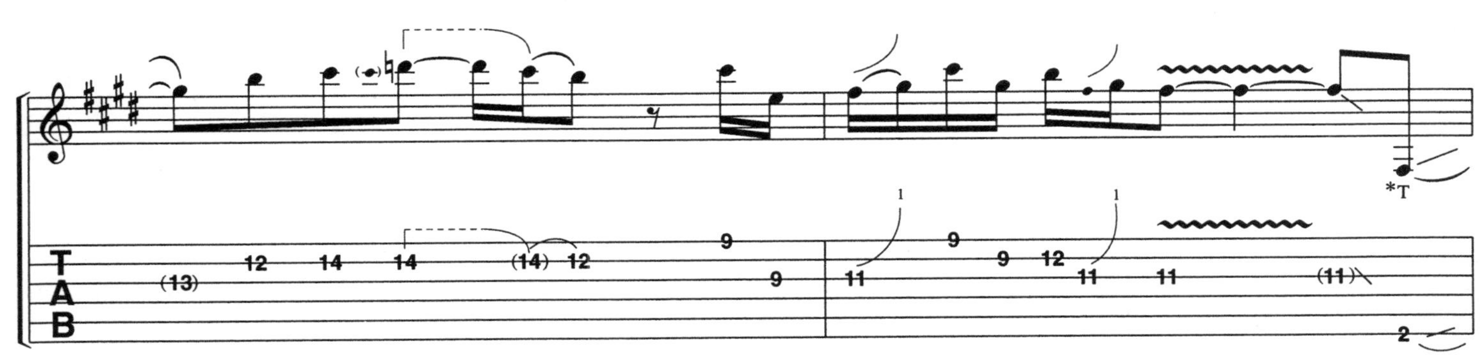

*slide up neck w/thumb of fret hand.

Gtr. 1
A
hold
T
Gtr. 2
P.M.
Gtr. 3
w/slight P.M.
E5
tr

E5
A
P.M.
P.M.
P.M.
P.M.
w/slight P.M.
E5
N.C.
A
G5
hold
hold
hold
hold
rit.
pick sl.
P.M.
P.M.
rit.
w/slight P.M.
rit.

*Verse 2:*
Eager for action, and hot for the game,
The coming attraction, the drop of a name.
They knew all the right people, they took the right pills,
They threw outrageous parties, they paid heavily bills.
There were lines on the mirror, lines on her face.
She pretended not to notice, she was caught up in the race.
Out ev'ry evenin' until it was light,
He was too tired to make it, she was too tired to fight about it.
*(To Chorus:)*

*Verse 3:*
Blowin' and burnin', blinded by thirst,
They didn't see the stop sign, took a turn for the worst.
She said, "Listen, baby. You can hear them engines ring.
We've been up and down the highway, haven't seen a god damn thing."
He said, "Call the doctor. I think I'm gonna crash."
And the doctor say he's comin', but you got to pay in cash.
They went rushin' down that freeway. Mess around and got lost.
They didn't know, they were just dyin' to get off and it was
*(To Chorus:)*

# desperado

Words and Music by
DON HENLEY and GLENN FREY

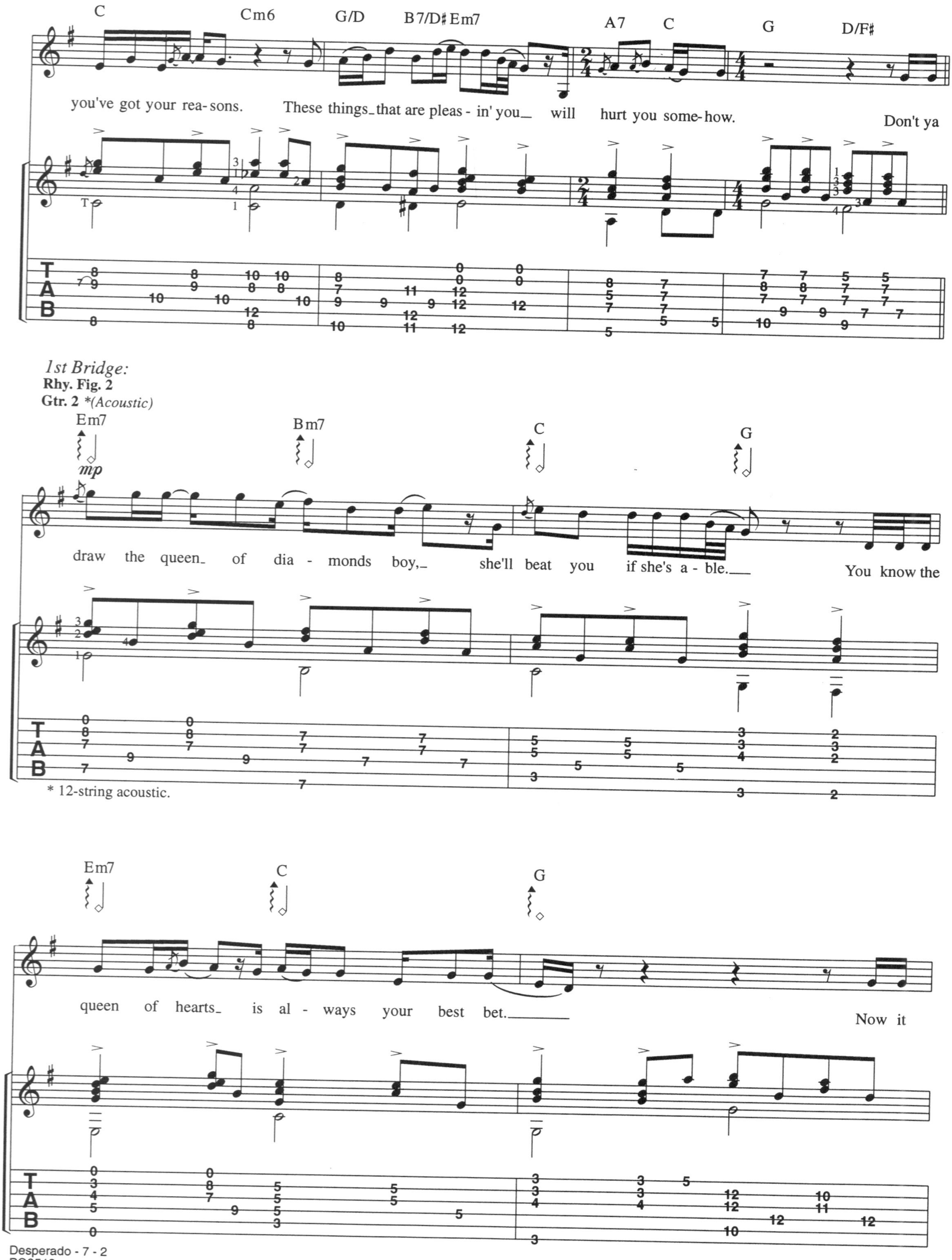

C Cm6 G/D B7/D♯ Em7 A7 C G D/F♯

you've got your rea-sons. These things_that are pleas - in' you_ will hurt you some-how. Don't ya

*1st Bridge:*

**Rhy. Fig. 2**

**Gtr. 2** **(Acoustic)*

Em7 Bm7 C G

*mp*

draw the queen_ of dia - monds boy,_ she'll beat you if she's a - ble.___ You know the

* 12-string acoustic.

Em7
Bm7
C
G
end Rhy. Fig. 2
seems to me some fine things have been laid up-on your ta-ble. But ya
end Rhy. Fig. 2a
Em7
A7
D7sus
D7
(Gtr. 2 out)
on-ly want the ones that you can't get. Des-per-a-
Verse 2;
w/Rhy. Fig. 1 simile (Gtr. I)
G
G7sus
C
-do, Oh, you ain't get-tin' no young-er. Your
Ooh,
Gtr. 3
mp vib. w/bar (throughout)

G D/F♯ Em7 A7 D7
pain and your hun - ger, they're driv - in' you home. And
Ooh.
G G7sus C
free-dom, oh free-dom, well that's just some peo-ple talk - in'. Your
Ooh.
hold mf
G/D B7/F♯ Em7 A7 D7 G D
pris-on is walk - in' through this world all a - lone. Don't your
Ooh.
mp
mf
hold
Bridge 2: Figs. 2&2A simile (Gtrs. 1 and 2)
Em7 Bm7 C G D/F♯
feet get cold in the win-ter time? The sky wants snow and the sun won't shine. It's
Aah.
mp

Em7
C
G
D/F♯
hard to tell the night-time from the day.
You're
mf
hold
Em7
Bm7
C
G
los - in' all your highs an' lows, Ain't it fun - ny how the feel - in' goes a -
Aah.
mp
Gtr. 2
Am7
D7sus
D
(Gtr. 2 out)
way?
Des - per - a -
Gtr. 1
Gtr. 3
mf
hold
hold
hold

Verse 3:
w/Rhy. Fig. 1 simile Gtr. 1 (1st 7 bars only)
G G7sus C Cm6 G B7/F♯ Em
- do, why don't you come to your sen - ses? Come down from your fence and
Ooh. Ooh.
hold
A7 D7 G G/A Bm7(♭5)
o - pen the gate. It may be rain - in; but there's a
Ooh.
C Cm6 G B7/F♯ Em
rain - bow a - bove you. You bet - ter let some - bod - y love you.
hold

C
Am7
(Gtr. 2 out)
G/D
B7/D♯
Em
Gtr. 2
You_ bet- ter let some - bod - y love___ you_______ be -
(let some - bod - y love______ you.)
Harm.
Gtr. 1
rit.
Harm.
Gtr. 3
(Gtr. 3 out)
rit.
Freely
D7sus
a tempo
G
G13
C
Gm6
G
Gtr. 2
fore it's too_______________ late_______________________
Gtr. 1
8va
rit.
Harm.

# GUITAR TAB GLOSSARY **

## TABLATURE EXPLANATION

**READING TABLATURE:** Tablature illustrates the six strings of the guitar. Notes and chords are indicated by the placement of fret numbers on a given string(s).

## BENDING NOTES

**HALF STEP:** Play the note and bend string one half step.*

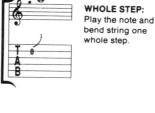

**WHOLE STEP:** Play the note and bend string one whole step.

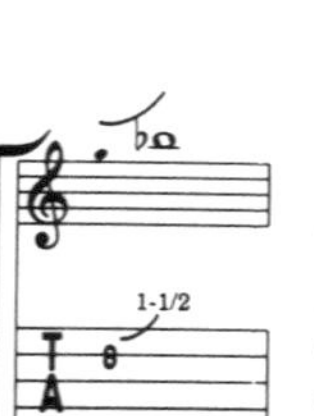

**WHOLE STEP AND A HALF:** Play the note and bend string a whole step and a half.

**SLIGHT BEND (Microtone):** Play the note and bend string slightly to the equivalent of half a fret.

*A half step is the smallest interval in Western music; it is equal to one fret. A whole step equals two frets.

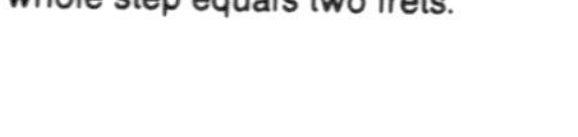

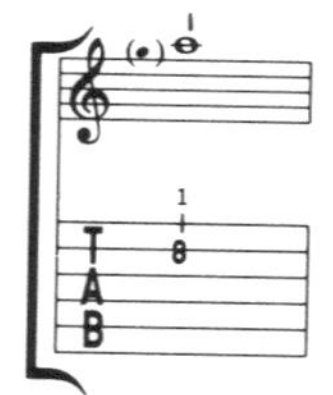

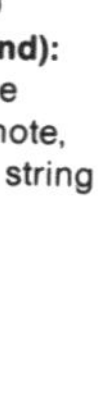

**PREBEND (Ghost Bend):** Bend to the specified note, before the string is picked.

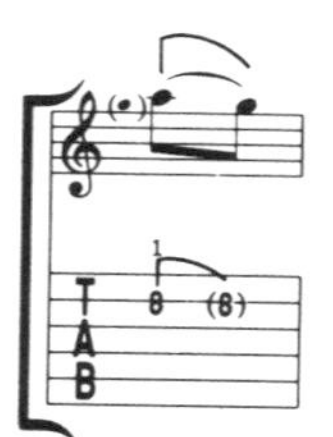

**PREBEND AND RELEASE:** Bend the string, play it, then release to the original note.

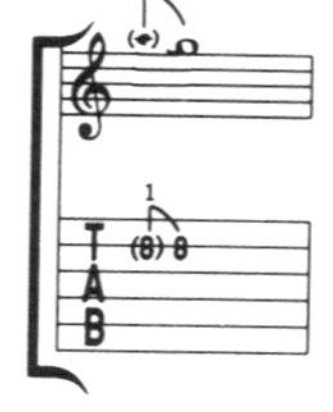

**REVERSE BEND:** Play the already-bent string, then immediately drop it down to the fretted note.

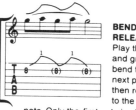

**BEND AND RELEASE:** Play the note and gradually bend to the next pitch, then release to the original note. Only the first note is attacked.

**UNISON BEND:** Play both notes and immediately bend the lower note to the same pitch as the higher note.

**DOUBLE NOTE BEND:** Play both notes and immediately bend both strings simultaneously.

**BENDS INVOLVING MORE THAN ONE STRING:** Play the note and bend string while playing an additional note (or notes) on another string(s). Upon release, relieve pressure from additional note(s), causing original note to sound alone.

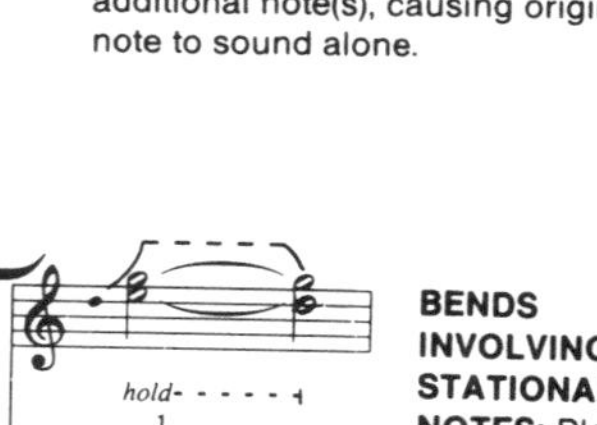

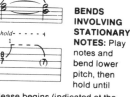

**BENDS INVOLVING STATIONARY NOTES:** Play notes and bend lower pitch, then hold until release begins (indicated at the point where line becomes solid).

## TREMOLO BAR

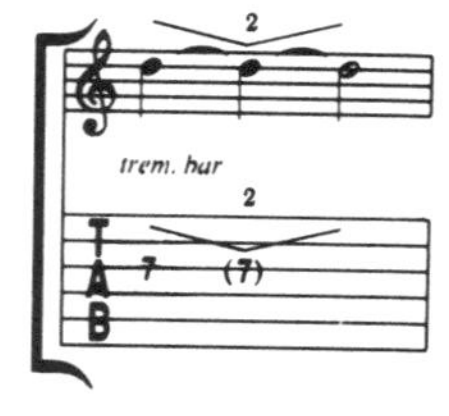

**SPECIFIED INTERVAL:** The pitch of a note or chord is lowered to a specified interval and then may or may not return to the original pitch. The activity of the tremolo bar is graphically represented by peaks and valleys.

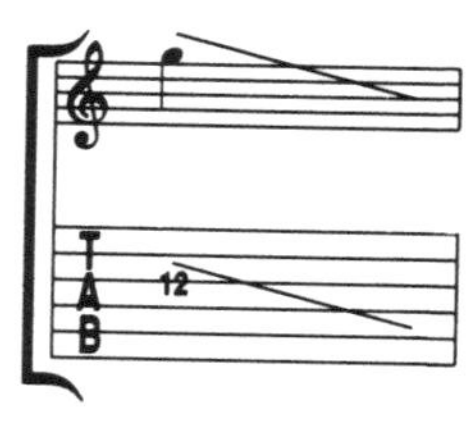

**UN-SPECIFIED INTERVAL:** The pitch of a note or a chord is lowered to an unspecified interval.

## HARMONICS

**NATURAL HARMONIC:** A finger of the fret hand lightly touches the note or notes indicated in the tab and is played by the pick hand.

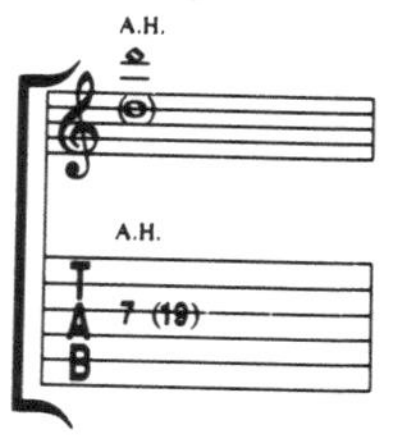

**ARTIFICIAL HARMONIC:** The first tab number is fretted, then the pick hand produces the harmonic by using a finger to lightly touch the same string at the second tab number (in parenthesis) and is then picked by another finger.

**ARTIFICIAL "PINCH" HARMONIC:** A note is fretted as indicated by the tab, then the pick hand produces the harmonic by squeezing the pick firmly while using the tip of the index finger in the pick attack. If parenthesis are found around the fretted note, it does not sound. No parenthesis means both the fretted note and A.H. are heard simultaneously.



**By Kenn Chipkin and Aaron Stang

## RHYTHM SLASHES

**STRUM INDICATIONS:** Strum with indicated rhythm.

The chord voicings are found on the first page of the transcription underneath the song title.

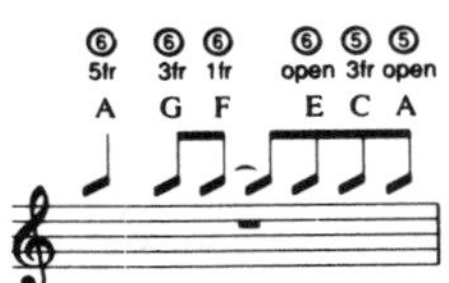


**INDICATING SINGLE NOTES USING RHYTHM SLASHES:** Very often single notes are incorporated into a rhythm part. The note name is indicated above the rhythm slash with a fret number and a string indication.

## ARTICULATIONS

**HAMMER ON:** Play lower note, then "hammer on" to higher note with another finger. Only the first note is attacked.

**LEFT HAND HAMMER:** Hammer on the first note played on each string with the left hand.

**PULL OFF:** Play higher note, then "pull off" to lower note with another finger. Only the first note is attacked.

**FRETBOARD TAPPING:** "Tap" onto the note indicated by + with a finger of the pick hand, then pull off to the following note held by the fret hand.

**TAP SLIDE:** Same as fretboard tapping, but the tapped note is slid randomly up the fretboard, then pulled off to the following note.

**BEND AND TAP TECHNIQUE:** Play note and bend to specified interval. While holding bend, tap onto note indicated.

**LEGATO SLIDE:** Play note and slide to the following note. (Only first note is attacked).

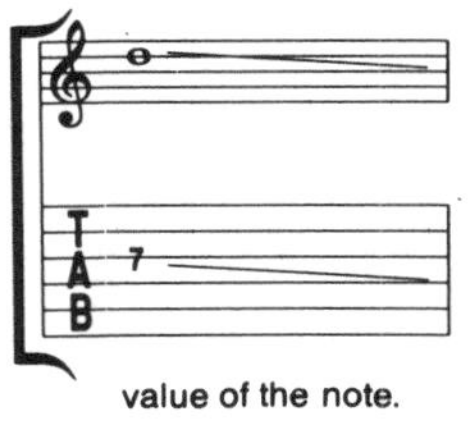

**LONG GLISSANDO:** Play note and slide in specified direction for the full value of the note.

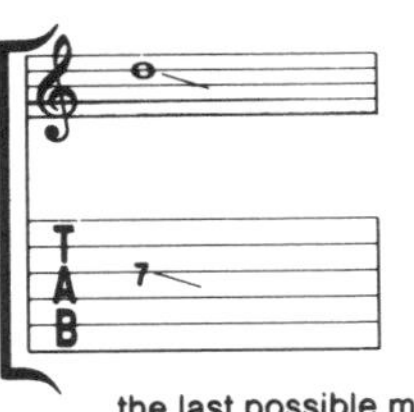

**SHORT GLISSANDO:** Play note for its full value and slide in specified direction at the last possible moment.

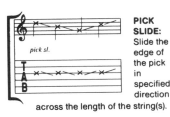

**PICK SLIDE:** Slide the edge of the pick in specified direction across the length of the string(s).

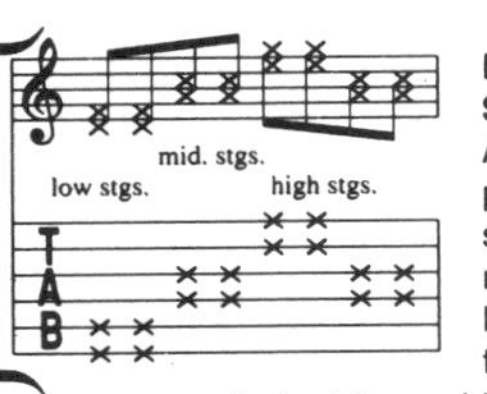
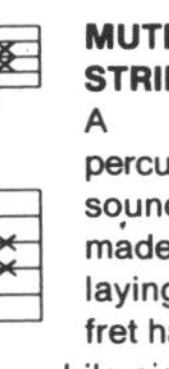


**MUTED STRINGS:** A percussive sound is made by laying the fret hand across all six strings while pick hand strikes specified area (low, mid, high strings).

**PALM MUTE:** The note or notes are muted by the palm of the pick hand by lightly touching the string(s) near the bridge.

**TREMOLO PICKING:** The note or notes are picked as fast as possible.

**TRILL:** Hammer on and pull off consecutively and as fast as possible between the original note and the grace note.

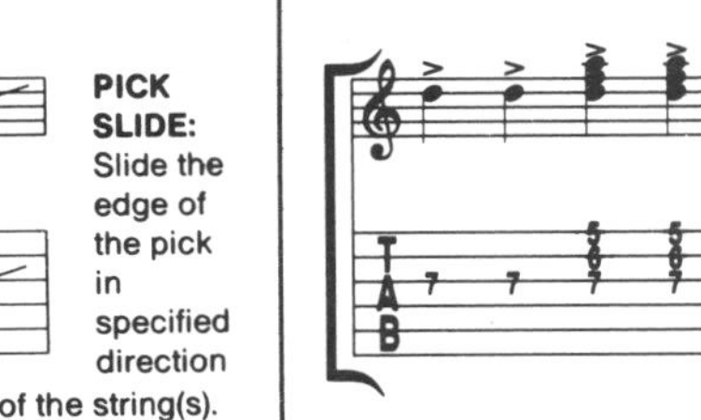

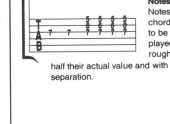

**ACCENT:** Notes or chords are to be played with added emphasis.

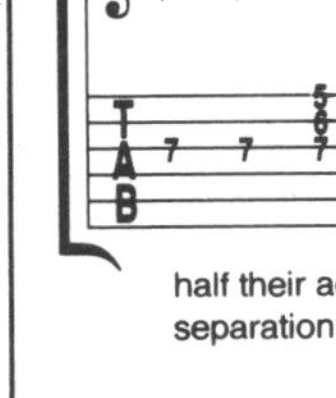

**STACCATO (Detached Notes):** Notes or chords are to be played roughly half their actual value and with separation.

**DOWN STROKES AND UPSTROKES:** Notes or chords are to be played with either a downstroke ( ⊓ ) or upstroke ( v ) of the pick.

**VIBRATO:** The pitch of a note is varied by a rapid shaking of the fret hand finger, wrist, and forearm.